The Ubiquity of Positive Measures for Addressing Systemic Discrimination and Inequality

Comparative Discrimination Law

Volumes published in this Brill Research Perspective are listed at *brill.com/rpcd*

The Ubiquity of Positive Measures for Addressing Systemic Discrimination and Inequality

A Comparative Global Perspective

By

David B. Oppenheimer

BRILL

LEIDEN | BOSTON

This paperback book edition is simultaneously published as issue 3.3–4 (2019) of *Comparative Discrimination Law*, DOI 10.1163/24522031-12340007.

Library of Congress Control Number: 2019945830

Typeface for the Latin, Greek, and Cyrillic scripts: "Brill". See and download: brill.com/brill-typeface.

ISBN 978-90-04-34598-0 (paperback)
ISBN 978-90-04-34599-7 (e-book)

This book is printed on acid-free paper and produced in a sustainable manner.

Contents

The Ubiquity of Positive Measures for Addressing Systemic Discrimination and Inequality

A Comparative Global Perspective

David B. Oppenheimer
University of California, Berkeley, USA
doppenheimer@law.berkeley.edu

Abstract

In *The Ubiquity of Positive Measures for Addressing Systemic Discrimination and Inequality: A Comparative Global Perspective*, part of the Brill series on *Comparative Discrimination Law*, David Oppenheimer compares positive measures for addressing inequality and systemic discrimination, including discrimination based on gender, race, ethnicity, color, national origin, disability, and religion. Across the globe, such measures are ubiquitous, commonly applied in employment, admission to selective colleges and universities, selection for legislative seats, and membership on corporate boards. They are variously described as "positive measures," "affirmative action," "positive action," "compensatory action," or "special measures."

These policies began in the late-eighteenth to mid-nineteenth centuries, as a part of the social/political movements to end slavery, grant universal suffrage, end colonialism, grant equal rights to women and men regardless of social status or property, eliminate the caste system, adopt measures of proportional representation, embrace the benefits of diversity, and endorse universal equality.

Nearly every large nation in the world has adopted at least some special measure plans, with continuing experiments using quotas, reservations, set-asides, reparations, preferences, tie-breakers, targeted recruiting efforts, diversity measures, equity and inclusion policies, anti or unconscious bias training, and public disclosure requirements.

Keywords

positive measures – positive action – affirmative action – anti-discrimination law – inequality – quotas – diversity – comparative equality – comparative anti-discrimination law – equity and inclusion

 | DOI:10.1163/9789004345997_002

Introduction

This monograph compares positive measures for addressing inequality and systemic discrimination, including discrimination based on gender, race, ethnicity, color, national origin, disability, and religion.[1] Across the globe, such measures are ubiquitous, commonly applied to employment hiring, admission to selective colleges and universities, selection for legislative seats, and membership on corporate boards. They may take the form of quotas, preferences, outreach programs, self-examination programs, and affirmative anti-discrimination efforts, sometimes including diversity, equity, and inclusion policies.[2] They are variously described as "positive measures," "affirmative action," "positive action," "compensatory action," or "special measures."[3] In discussing them, I will generally use the term used by the national or international legal system under discussion, but when discussing the generic idea of positive measures, I will usually use either the term "positive measures" or the U.S. term, "affirmative action."

The roots of the world-wide movement for positive measures arose in the late eighteenth and early nineteenth centuries, as part of the social movements against inequality, monarchy/aristocracy, colonialism, and slavery. The American and French revolutions declared a commitment to equality that spread throughout the world. As the successes of the anti-slavery movement, the women's suffrage/rights movement, and the anti-colonialism movement grew in the 19th century, societies across the globe were forced to confront the question of how to remedy past discrimination and structural disadvantage. In the United States, the debates over post-Civil War Reconstruction were, in significant part, debates over positive measures. Some of those who opposed positive measures did so because they favored white male supremacy and opposed the liberation of slaves or equality rights for women and/or racial/ethnic minorities. But even among those who supported equality, there was a division over whether to support race-conscious positive measures. For example, two great Black American abolitionists, Frederick Douglass and Martin Delany,

---

1 There are, of course, many other forms of systemic discrimination, including sexual orientation, gender identity, age, and point-of-view discrimination, which are serious social problems, and are often the subject of anti-discrimination laws, but not commonly addressed through positive measures.

2 See David B. Oppenheimer, "Distinguishing Five Models of Affirmative Action," *Berkeley Women's Law Journal* 4, no. 1 (1988): 43–50.

3 Christopher McCrudden, "A Comparative Taxonomy of 'Positive Action' and 'Affirmative Action' Policies," *Queen's University Belfast Law Research Paper* 12, no. 4 (2012): 157–158.

together published a leading abolitionist newspaper, the North Star, but fiercely disagreed about whether reparations, job quotas, legislative quotas, and other positive measures for the newly freed slaves should be instituted.[4]

Similarly, in Britain, advocates for universal suffrage proposed new voting systems replacing a plurality/majority selection process with proportional representation, to offer some protection to the existing male land-owning class while expanding the franchise.[5] This idea of proportional representation, popularized in England by John Stuart Mill as both a means of measuring discrimination (when representation is disproportionate) and a remedy for discrimination, is now found at the heart of positive measures.[6]

In India, Chhatrapati Shahu, the Maharaja of Kolhapur, reserved 50% of government positions for members of "backwards classes" in 1902, for which he became known as "the father of reservations."[7] By 1906, Shahu established a universal primary education system and schools specifically designed to help those denied access to education by the Hindu majority.[8] Shahu also sought to promote equality amongst all strata of society by establishing the Deccan Rayat Association in 1916 to secure political rights for non-Brahmins, ordering his subjects to treat every member of the society as equal, legalizing inter-caste marriages, and granting the "untouchables" equal access to public utilities, schools, and hospitals.[9] For the sake of gender equality, Shahu established schools for women, banned the practice of offering girls to God, which essentially led to the exploitation of girls at the hands of the Clergy, legalized widow remarriages, and attempted to stop

---

4 Morris B. Abrams, "Affirmative Action: Fair Shakers and Social Engineers," *Harvard Law Review* 99, no. 6 (1986): 1314–1315; Robert S. Levine, *Martin R. Delany: A Documentary Reader*, (Chapel Hill: University of North Carolina Press, 2003), 380.

5 Thomas Hare, *Election of Representatives, Parliamentary and Municipal*. 4th ed. (London: Longmans, Green, Reader, & Dyer, 1873), v.

6 John S. Mill, *Considerations on Representative Government*, (London: Parker, Son, & Bourn, 1861), 64–69, 152–158.

7 Nagpur Today, "Meritorious X, XII Students Honoured by BSP," Nagpur Today Nagpur News RSS. July 27, 2015, accessed January 18, 2019. https://www.nagpurtoday.in/meritorious-x-xii-students-honoured-by-bsp/07271411.

8 Abhiram Ghadyalpatil, "Rajarshi Shahu Chhatrapati of Kolhapur, a Reformer Ahead of His Time," Livement.com. August 10, 2018, accessed January 18, 2019. https://www.livemint.com/Leisure/PLkr7jdpCeZepho8RMVJbN/Rajarshi-Shahu-Chhatrapati-of-Kolhapur-a-reformer-ahead-of.html.

9 Cultural India, "Life History of Shahu Chhatrapati," *Biography – Life History, Facts, Achievements & Death*. May 15, 2016, accessed January 18, 2019. https://www.culturalindia.net/reformers/shahu-chhatrapati.html.

child marriages.[10] Unfortunately upon Shahu's death in 1922, many of his reforms were gradually rolled back under the reign of his successors.[11]

This debate over positive measures – then and now – was and remains often framed as a choice between formal equality and substantive equality. Supporters of formal equality generally opposed positive measures, asserting that they are a form of discrimination, or "reverse discrimination." Supporters of substantive equality respond that the accumulated disadvantage of inequality, and the effect of negative stereotypes and continuing discrimination, can only be eradicated through positive measures. Thus, American President Lyndon Johnson argued:

> You do not wipe away the scars of centuries by saying: Now you are free to go where you want, and do as you desire, and choose the leaders you please. You do not take a person who, for years, has been hobbled by chains and liberate him, bring him up to the starting line of a race and then say, "you are free to compete with all the others," and still justly believe that you have been completely fair. Thus it is not enough just to open the gates of opportunity. All our citizens must have the ability to walk through those gates.[12]

In examining this debate, it is sometimes hard to determine when the formal equality position is held by persons who truly oppose discrimination against disadvantaged groups, and when it is a cynical means of promoting white male supremacy behind the cover of supporting the anti-discrimination principle.

While the roots of positive measure policies are found in the eighteenth and nineteenth centuries, the policies saw broad adoption in the twentieth. In the wake of the first World War, several European powers, including France and Germany, adopted hiring quotas for disabled veterans.[13] Over time, these quotas were extended to all persons with disabilities, or at least all who registered with the state.[14] And as disability law moved from a social welfare model to

10 Ibid.

11 Ibid.

12 Lyndon B. Johnson, "To Fulfill These Rights," Speech, Howard University Commencement Address, Howard University, Washington D.C., June 4, 1965.

13 *See* Lisa Waddington, "Disability: A Human Rights Issue," *Maastricht Journal of European and Comparative Law* 1, no. 4 (December 1994): 334–336. doi:10.1177/1023263X9400100401.

14 Ibid.

an anti-discrimination model, in many cases the quotas were retained as anti-discrimination positive measures programs.[15]

At around the same time as European powers were instituting hiring quotas for disabled veterans, Black Americans were beginning to organize boycotts of employers who refused to hire Black workers, demanding of their neighbors, "Don't Shop Where You Can't Work."[16] Such boycotts continued into the 1960s, when a nationwide boycott campaign for affirmative action was led by the Rev. Dr. Martin Luther King, Jr.[17]

And again in the period just following World War I, Britain began adopting quota programs in India to promote representation in public employment, education, and political offices for lower Caste Indians and Muslims.

Then, in the wake of the second World War and the Holocaust, a growing world-wide opposition to discrimination developed, accompanied by broad adoptions of positive measures.[18] Positive action was provided for in the international conventions prohibiting racial discrimination and gender discrimination.[19] In recognition of the division between substantive equality arguments for and formal equality arguments against such measures, the conventions permitted, but did not require, positive measures.[20] And, they limited such actions to equalizing participation, but not perpetuating it.[21] Regional conventions also incorporated positive measures, including the European treaties that began as a six-nation steel and coal pact, and are today the core of the 28-member European Union.[22]

---

15 *See* Lisa Waddington, "The relationship between Disability Non-Discrimination Law and Quota Schemes: A comparison between Common Law and Civil Law Jurisdictions in Europe," at 1–2, in *Anti-Discrimination Law in Civil Law Jurisdictions*, ed. Barbara Havelkova and Mathias Moschel (Oxford: Oxford University Press, (forthcoming)).

16 *See* David B. Oppenheimer, "Dr. King's Dream of Affirmative Action," *Harvard Latinx Law Review* 21, 56 (2018): 63–70.

17 Ibid.

18 Waddington, "The relationship between Disability Non-Discrimination Law and Quota Schemes," 3.

19 *See generally* International Convention on the Elimination of All Forms of Racial Discrimination, 21 December 1965, 94 U.T.S. 1120, 660 U.N.T.S. 195; *See also generally* Convention on the Elimination of All Forms of Discrimination Against Women, 18 December 1979, 1249 U.N.T.S. 13.

20 ICERD, art. 2.2, 21 December 1965, 94 U.T.S. 1120, 660 U.N.T.S. 195; CEDAW, art. 1.4, 18 December 1979, 1249 U.N.T.S. 13.

21 ICERD, art. 1.4, 21 December 1965, 94 U.T.S. 1120, 660 U.N.T.S. 195; CEDAW, art. 2, 18 December 1979, 1249 U.N.T.S. 13.

22 *See* Waddington, "The relationship between Disability Non-Discrimination Law and Quota Schemes," 3–4.

As described in the parts that follow, it was in this post-war period, and the rights revolution that followed, that positive measures became an important part of public policy in the United States, India, Canada, Colombia, Brazil, South Africa, across Europe, and elsewhere. But the near-universal adoption of positive measures has been accompanied nearly everywhere by tension, push-back, and backlash, as opponents argue that positive measures are simply a form of discrimination. The question often comes down to whether these efforts are examined through the lens of formal equality or substantive equality.

For example, in the 1987 case *CN v. Canada (Canadian Human Rights Commission)*, the Supreme Court of Canada unanimously reinstated a Tribal Order requiring the Canadian National Railway to hire one woman for every four entries into its unskilled, blue-collar labor force.[23] In its ruling, the Court stated: "[a]n employment equity program, such as the one in the present case, is designed to break a continuing cycle of systemic discrimination. The goal is not to compensate past victims or even to provide new opportunities for specific individuals who have been unfairly refused jobs or promotion in the past. Rather, an employment equity program is an attempt to ensure that future applicants and workers from the affected group will not face the same insidious barriers that blocked their forebears. In any employment equity program, there simply cannot be a radical dissociation of 'remedy' and 'prevention' for there is no prevention without some form of remedy."[24] The Canadian court was embracing a substantive equality approach to the issue.

By contrast, the United States Supreme Court, choosing a formal equality model, rejected a plan by the Seattle Washington School Board to promote integration in its formerly segregated schools by giving enrollment preferences to students whose presence in a school would make it more racially or ethnically diverse. Chief Justice John Roberts rejected the plan as discriminatory, announcing that "The way to stop discrimination on the basis of race is to stop discriminating on the basis of race."[25]

In the pages that follow, I will review and compare how positive measures for addressing systemic discrimination and inequality have developed across the globe in four fields: employment, access to higher education, democratic elections, and corporate board membership.

---

23 *CN v. Canada (Canadian Human Rights Commission)*, [1987] 1 S.C.R. 1114, 1131 (Can.).

24 Ibid., at 1116.

25 *Parents Involved in Cmty. Sch. v. Seattle Sch. Dist. No. 1*, 551 U.S. 701, 748 (2007).

Part 1: Positive Measures and Labor/Employment Law

Although the roots of the world-wide movement for positive measures arose in the late eighteenth and early nineteenth centuries as part of the social movements against inequality, monarchy/aristocracy, colonialism, and slavery, the law of positive measures in employment was first developed in the labor laws meant to enable wounded veterans to gain employment in the wake of World War I, through the use of a quota system.[26] With time these employment quota systems grew to become part of a holistic program meant to promote a more just society in general.[27] The form of affirmative action employment programs ranges from hard quota systems for disadvantaged groups, through various systems described herein to reduce discrimination and promote diversity, to soft voluntary inclusion programs. Along this continuum, the closer we get to the hard quota laws, the greater the opposition. That opposition often relies on the argument that special measures that advantaged members of a disadvantaged racial, religious, gender, or ethnic group violate the anti-discrimination principle. A frequent response is that the anti-discrimination principle should be applied in light of the realities of discrimination and inequality. These two camps are widely described as the formal equality camp and the substantive equality camp. The approach of several states and international conventions combines a concession that a system of permanent or perpetual quotas would violate the anti-discrimination principle, with an embrace of their adoption as a temporary remedy to inequality and discrimination. It is in the field of employment law that these arguments are most often confronted. Accordingly, and in light of the wide array of approaches to affirmative action in employment, this book begins by comparing different approaches to affirmative action/positive measures in employment.

1.1 *Positive Measures in International Law*

In the wake of the Holocaust/Shoah, the world turned far greater attention to the problem of racism and incorporated the fight against racism into the formation of the United Nations. The International Convention on the Elimination of All Forms of Racial Discrimination (ICERD),[28] which was proposed in 1963 and adopted through the United Nations in 1965, includes two

26 Waddington, "The relationship between Disability Non-Discrimination Law and Quota Schemes," 2–3.

27 Ibid.

28 *See generally* ICERD, 21 December 1965, 94 U.T.S. 1120, 660 U.N.T.S. 195.

articles that deal specifically with positive measures. These measures confront head-on the argument that positive measures violate the anti-discrimination principle. First, the ICERD provides that positive measures shall not be treated as a form of discrimination, but second, it further provides that they remain in place only as long as necessary. The Convention, thus, endorses the substantive equality argument that positive measures promote (not violate) the anti-discrimination principle. But in doing so, there is a nod to concerns about positive measures creating a long-term quota system instead of a process for countering discrimination and inequality and a concession that a perpetual quota system would violate the anti-discrimination principle. Article 1.4 permits the adoption of "special measures" to fight discrimination, providing:

> Special measures taken for the sole purpose of securing adequate advancement of certain racial or ethnic groups or individuals requiring such protection as may be necessary in order to ensure such groups or individuals equal enjoyment or exercise of human rights and fundamental freedoms shall not be deemed racial discrimination, provided, however, that such measures do not, as a consequence, lead to the maintenance of separate rights for different racial groups and that they shall not be continued after the objectives for which they were taken have been achieved.[29]

Article 2.2 obliges States to adopt affirmative action in social, economic, cultural, and other fields when the circumstances so provide. The obligation applies to both private and public spheres. Here again, there is an endorsement of positive measures tempered by a nod to concerns about creating a long-term quota system instead of a process for countering discrimination and inequality.

> States Parties shall, when the circumstances so warrant, take, in the social, economic, cultural and other fields, special and concrete measures to ensure the adequate development and protection of certain racial groups or individuals belonging to them, for the purpose of guaranteeing them the full and equal enjoyment of human rights and fundamental freedoms. These measures shall in no case entail as a consequence the maintenance of unequal or separate rights for different racial groups after the objectives for which they were taken have been achieved.[30]

29 Ibid. at Article 1.4.
30 Ibid. at Article 2.2.

According to the United Nations Development Program (UNDP), "the use of the verb 'shall' clearly indicates the mandatory nature of the obligation" of States to adopt such measures to correct imbalances in the enjoyment of human rights.[31] The Committee also states that "it is not necessary to prove such 'historic' discrimination in order to validate a programme of special measures; [but rather] the emphasis should be placed on correcting present disparities and on preventing further imbalances from arising."[32]

The Committee on the Elimination of Racial Discrimination (CERD) is the body monitoring States' compliance with the Convention. All States are obliged to submit regular reports to the Committee on how the rights provided by the Convention are being implemented. The CERD Committee advises that "[s]pecial measures should be appropriate to the situation to be remedied, be legitimate, necessary in a democratic society, respect the principles of fairness and proportionality, and be temporary."[33] Here again, the expectation is that positive measures will be remedial, and thus, temporary.

The Convention on the Elimination of All Forms of Discrimination against Women (CEDAW),[34] adopted in 1979 by the UN General Assembly, is often described as an international bill of rights for women.[35] The Convention provides the basis for realizing equality between women and men through ensuring women's equal access to, and equal opportunities in, political and public life – including the right to vote and to stand for election – as well as to education, health, and employment. CEDAW places clear obligations on State parties to adopt proper legislative measures, to establish legal protections for women, and to ensure that public authorities act in conformity with this obligation.[36] With regard to positive measures, Article 4.1 states that:

> Adoption by States Parties of temporary special measures aimed at accelerating de facto equality between men and women shall not be

31 UN Comm. on the Elimination of Racial Discrimination (CERD), General Recommendation No. 32, The meaning and scope of special measures in the Int'l Convention on the Elimination of All Forms [of] Racial Discrimination, par. 30, CERD/C/GC/32 (September 24, 2009).

32 UN Comm. on the Elimination of Racial Discrimination (CERD), Report of the Comm. on the Elimination of Racial Discrimination: Seventy-fifth session (3–28 August 2009), Annex Seven para. 21–22, A/64/18 (December 21, 2011).

33 CERD, "General Recommendation No. 32," para. 16.

34 *See generally* CEDAW, 18 December 1979, 1249 U.N.T.S. 13.

35 Laura Carlson, *Comparative Discrimination Law: Historical and Theoretical Frameworks* (Leiden: Brill 2017), 7–10, doi:10.1163/9789004345454.

36 CEDAW, preamble, 18 December 1979, 1249 U.N.T.S. 13.

> considered discrimination as defined in the present Convention, but shall in no way entail as a consequence the maintenance of unequal or separate standards; these measures shall be discontinued when the objectives of equality of opportunity and treatment have been achieved.[37]

The language of this section thus establishes not only that promoting gender equality through positive measures is permitted, but also that the formal equality argument – that affirmative action is itself discrimination – is rejected.

The United Nations Convention on the Rights of Persons With Disabilities (CRPD), adopted by the United Nations in 2006, and ratified by 177 States (but not including the United States), requires State signatories to promote, protect, and ensure the full and equal enjoyment of all human rights and fundamental freedoms by all persons with disabilities.[38] Article 5(4) states that "[s]pecific measures which are necessary to accelerate or achieve de facto equality of persons with disabilities shall not be considered discrimination under the terms of the present Convention."[39] Affirmative action specific to work and employment is found in Article 27, which states:

> States Parties recognize the right of persons with disabilities to work, on an equal basis with others; this includes the right to the opportunity to gain a living by work freely chosen or accepted in a labour market and work environment that is open, inclusive and accessible to persons with disabilities. States Parties shall safeguard and promote the realization of the right to work, including for those who acquire a disability during the course of employment, by taking appropriate steps, including through legislation, to, inter alia: ... (h) Promote the employment of persons with disabilities in the private sector through appropriate policies and measures, which may include affirmative action programmes, incentives and other measures.[40]

Here again, the formal equality argument that affirmative action is a form of discrimination is rejected, and the treaty requires it when necessary to promote equality.

---

37 Ibid. at article 4.1.

38 Convention on the Rights of Persons with Disabilities: resolution / adopted by the General Assembly, Annex 1 preamble, 24 January 2007, 2515 U.N.T.S. 3, A/RES/61/106.

39 Ibid. at article 5(4).

40 Ibid. at article 27.

As an example of the reach of the CRPD, when its Committee on the Rights of Persons with Disabilities expressed concerns "about the high unemployment rate of persons with disabilities" in China as well as the average salary rank of Chinese people with disabilities that fell "well below that of persons without disabilities,"[41] the Committee recommended that China "introduce affirmative actions to promote the employment of persons with disabilities, inter alia, to prioritize the employment of persons with disabilities as civil servants."[42]

The CRPD also provides that the failure to make reasonable accommodations to persons with disabilities is, itself, a form of discrimination.[43] One might characterize this obligation as a form of positive measure, but the emerging view is that it is better understood to reside entirely within the definition of discrimination.[44] The reasoning is that the lack of reasonable accommodations is, itself, a form of discrimination against people with disabilities.[45] Accordingly, requiring reasonable accommodations is not affirmative action as it is not a positive measure; it is a requirement that employers must cease discriminating.[46]

The International Covenant on Economic, Social and Cultural Rights (ICESCR) provides in Article 2.1 that "[e]ach State Party to the present Covenant undertakes to take steps, individually and through international assistance and co-operation, especially economic and technical, to the maximum of its available resources, with a view to achieving progressively the full realization of the rights recognized in the present Covenant by all appropriate means, including particularly the adoption of legislative measures."[47] The Committee on Economic, Social and Cultural Rights (CESCR) interprets the prohibition of discrimination in Articles 2 and 3 of the ICESCR. The core of the conception of anti-discrimination put forward by CESCR is that as discrimination undermines the fulfillment of economic, social, and cultural rights, non-discrimination

41 UN Committee on the Rights of Persons with Disabilities (CRPD), Concluding observations on the initial report of China, adopted by the Committee at its 8th session, 17–28 September 2012: Committee on the Rights of Persons with Disabilities, para. 77, CRPD/C/CHN/CO/1 (October 15, 2012).

42 Ibid. at para 78.

43 CRPD at art. 2.

44 *See* Waddington, "The relationship between Disability Non-Discrimination Law and Quota Schemes," 17–18, 22–23.

45 *See* Ibid.

46 *See* Ibid.

47 International Covenant on Economic, Social and Cultural Rights, art. 2.1, 16 December 1966, 993 U.N.T.S. 3.

and equality are fundamental components of international human rights law and essential to the enjoyment of the rights in the Covenant.

With regard to disability discrimination, the CESCR Committee's General Comments provide that States' obligation to promote the progressive realization of social, economic, and cultural rights to the maximum of their available resources, requires them not only to abstain from adopting measures that could negatively affect persons with disabilities, but also "to take positive action to reduce structural disadvantages and to give appropriate preferential treatment to people with disabilities in order to achieve the objectives of full participation and equality within society for all persons with disabilities."[48] General Comment No. 20 on Non-discrimination in 2009 provides that "[i]n order to eliminate substantive discrimination, States Parties may be, and in some cases are, under an obligation to adopt special measures to attenuate or suppress conditions that perpetuate discrimination."[49] Such positive measures may need to be of a permanent nature, such as interpretation services for linguistic minorities and reasonable accommodation of persons with sensory impairments in accessing health care facilities.[50]

The International Labor Organization (ILO) was created in 1919 as part of the Treaty of Versailles that ended World War I.[51] The ILO brings together governments, employers, and workers' representatives of 187 member States, to set labor standards, develop policies, and devise programs promoting decent work for all women and men.[52] The ILO Equal Remuneration Convention provides for non-discrimination at work, and more specifically, equality of pay on the basis of the principle of "equal remuneration for work of equal value" affirmed in the ILO Constitution.[53] This principle means that rates and types of remuneration should be based not on an employee's sex, but on an objective evaluation of the work performed.[54] Members, after consulting employers' and

48 CESCR, General Comment No. 5: Persons with Disabilities, par. 9, E/1995/22 (December 9, 1994),

49 CESCR, General Comment No. 20 par. 9.

50 Ibid. at para. 10.

51 International Labour Organization (ILO), Constitution of the International Labour Organisation (ILO), 1 April 1919; Carlson, *Comparative Discrimination Law: Historical and Theoretical Frameworks*, 7–10.

52 ILO, Constitution of the ILO at Annex 1; "Alphabetical List of ILO Member Countries," *ILO.Org*. Oct. 22, 2018, accessed Nov. 11, 2018. https://www.ilo.org/public/english/standards/relm/country.htm.

53 ILO, Constitution of the ILO at preamble.

54 International Labour Office, *ABC of Women Workers' Rights and Gender Equality* (Geneva: International Labour Organisation, 2000), 38.

workers' organizations, may determine special measures required for persons who, on grounds such as sex, age, disablement, family responsibility, social or cultural status, require such protection or assistance.[55]

In sum, across a broad swath of international labor and employment law, states are expected to adopt temporary measures to address discrimination and inequality, and to assure workplace equality to members of racial, ethnic, national origin, and religious minorities, to women, and to persons with disabilities. And in response to the formal equality argument against special measures, in each instance states are expected to protect against a system of perpetual quotas by providing that the special measures they adopt are temporary. How well they carry out these obligations through national law and practice will be addressed in the sections that follow.

1.2 *Positive Measures in Employment in the United States*

At the conclusion of the American Civil War (1865), the United States entered a period of "Reconstruction," in which slavery and state-imposed inequality were abolished by Constitutional amendment,[56] and policies were adopted to provide positive measures for the freed slaves to achieve legal, social, and economic equality. Professor Randall Kennedy argues that the Equal Protection guarantee of the 14th amendment is, itself, a form of affirmative action.[57] Congress established The Freedmen's Bureau[58] to reserve jobs and other economic opportunities for the newly freed African American population in the South.[59] The Freedmen's Bureau at times applied principles of proportional representation and positive measures to ensure opportunities to the freed slaves.[60] The desirability of positive measures was hotly debated, not only by the opponents of Reconstruction, but also by its supporters. The opponents of the positive measures, such as President Andrew Johnson, opposed it on both

---

55 *See* International Labour Organization (ILO), ILO Declaration on Fundamental Principles and Rights at Work, June 1988.

56 Eric Foner, *Reconstruction: America's unfinished revolution, 1863–1877* (New York: Harper Collins, 2011), 60–76; U.S. Const. amend. XIII (abolishing slavery) and XIV (guaranteeing equal protection of the laws).

57 Randall Kennedy, *For Discrimination: Race, Affirmative Action, and the Law* (New York: Penguin Random House, 2013), 22–25.

58 37th U.S. Congress. *Statutes at Large of the United States (1863–1865)*. Washington: Library of Congress, 1864. Vol. 13, p. 507. Foner, *Reconstruction: America's unfinished revolution, 1863–1877*, 68–70.

59 *See* George R. Bentley, *A History of the Freedmen's Bureau*. (Philadelphia: University of Pennsylvania Press, 1955): 46–49.

60 Foner, *Reconstruction: America's unfinished revolution, 1863–1877*, 60–76.

racist grounds and on the basis that it was showing African Americans undue favoritism.[61] Meanwhile the supporters of Reconstruction, such as Black abolitionists Frederick Douglass and Martin Delany, had a significant falling out over their respective positions, with Martin Delany calling for positive measures based on a principle of proportional representation, while Douglass insisted that race-blind non-discrimination was the best tool for ending inequality.[62]

Reconstruction ended with the Presidential election of 1876 and was followed by the "Jim Crow" era of ever-stricter racial segregation, as well as terrorist attacks on Black Americans by the Ku Klux Klan and other white supremacist groups. Employment opportunities for most Black Americans were extremely limited.[63] In the South, the largest share of the Black population lived in rural areas and worked as tenant farmers.[64] Near the end of the 19th century, Black Americans began migrating in large numbers to the North.[65] There, they mostly held the lowest paying and most difficult manual labor positions, as well as positions as servants, housekeepers, maids, janitors, and other service positions.[66] As late as "1978 most black professionals, administrators, and officials were concentrated in sectors that disproportionately served blacks."[67] In 1979, 99 percent of all minority business was based on sales to minority consumers or federal procurement.[68]

The first post-Reconstruction voluntary affirmative action programs, based on a principle of proportional representation, emerged in the 1920s, through a series of boycotts of businesses that were located in Black neighborhoods yet had few, if any, Black employees.[69] The boycotts were often the result of collaboration between the Black press and Black churches, with the cooperation of the newly emerging civil rights organizations such as the National Association for the Advancement of Colored People (NAACP) and the Urban

61 Kennedy, *For Discrimination: Race, Affirmative Action, and the Law*, 22–25.

62 Abrams, "Affirmative Action: Fair Shakers and Social Engineers," 1314–1315; Levine, "*Martin R. Delany: A Documentary Reader*, 380.

63 James N. Gregory, *The Southern Diaspora: How the Great Migrations of Black and White Southerners Transformed America* (Chapel Hill: University of North Carolina Press, 2006), 19.

64 Ibid. at 19; *see also generally* Isabel Wilkerson, *The Warmth of Other Suns: The Epic Story of Americas Great Migration* (New York: Vintage, 2010).

65 Gregory, *The Southern Diaspora*, 12–19.

66 Ibid. at 95–100.

67 Ibid. at 376.

68 Ibid. at 377.

69 Waldo E. Martin, Jr. and Patricia Sullivan, "'Don't Buy Where You Can't Work' Campaigns," *U.S. History in Context.* Accessed 29 Oct. 2017. link.galegroup.com/apps/doc/BT2338230739/UHIC?u=k12_histrc&xid=8c8bd1b6.

League.[70] The boycotts were often organized under the slogan "Don't Buy Where You Can't Work" and demanded the proportional hire of Black employees to end the boycott.[71] These boycotts had considerable success in the 1920s and 1930s and produced significant numbers of jobs based on the principle of proportional representation.[72] Two U.S. Supreme Court decisions, *New Negro Alliance v. Sanitary Grocery Co.*[73] and *NAACP v. Claiborne Hardware Co.*[74] held that boycotts to demand non-discrimination were lawfully protected under the labor laws, and later the First Amendment to the U.S. Constitution. However, a third case held that boycotts that demanded proportional hiring or quotas violated public policy.[75] That view was endorsed by the mainstream civil rights organizations, and particularly the NAACP, which in the 1950s were opposed to quotas and proportionate hiring in employment.[76] This position evolved over time; by the 1970s they were again important supporters of affirmative action, including quota-based hiring.[77]

There had also been government and corporate efforts beginning in the 1930s to encourage private employers to engage in affirmative action and to adopt anti-discrimination policies.[78] At times under the Roosevelt administration, there had been racial quotas used for some of the "New Deal" employment programs, yet in other instances the Roosevelt administration supported Jim Crow practices.[79] For example, the Public Works Administration ("PWA") required federal contractors on PWA projects to reserve a percentage of their

70 August Meier and Elliott Rudwick, "The Origins of Nonviolent Direct Action in Afro-American Protest: A Note on Historical Discontinuities," in *Along the Color Line: Explorations in the Black Experience*, edited by David Levering Lewis (Champaign: University of Illinois Press, 1976), 307–316.

71 Ibid.; Oppenheimer, "Dr. King's Dream of Affirmative Action," 63–70; David B. Oppenheimer, "The Disappearance of Voluntary Affirmative Action from the U.S. Workplace," *Journal of Poverty and Social Justice* 24, no. 1 (2016): 39–40.

72 Oppenheimer, "Dr. King's Dream of Affirmative Action," 63–70.

73 *See generally New Negro Alliance v. Sanitary Grocery Co.*, 303 U.S. 552 (1938).

74 *See generally NAACP v. Claiborne Hardware Co.*, 458 U.S. 886 (1982).

75 *See generally Hughes v. Superior Court*, 339 U.S. 460 (1950).

76 Ken Kersch, *Constructing Civil Liberties: Discontinuities in the Development of American Constitutional Law.* (Cambridge: Cambridge University Press, 2004), 217.

77 *See e.g., United Steelworkers v. Weber*, 443 U.S. 193 n.+ (1979) (Noting in a foot note the NAACP's support of affirmative action in this case).

78 Oppenheimer, "Dr. King's Dream of Affirmative Action," 63–70.

79 Ibid; Garth E. Pauley. "Harry Truman and the NAACP: A Case Study in Presidential Persuasion on Civil Rights," *Rhetoric and Public Affairs* 2, no. 2, Special Issue on Civil Rights in the Postmodern Era (1999): 216–218; Paul Moreno, "An Ambivalent Legacy: Black Americans and the Political Economy of the New Deal," *The Independent Review* 6, no. 4 (2002): 513–539; *see also generally* Richard Rothstein, *The Color of Law: A Forgotten History of How Our Government Segregated America* (New York: Liveright, 2017).

payroll for Black workers, and several other New Deal agencies experimented with distributing jobs or public benefits based on racial proportionality.[80] But at the same time, the Roosevelt administration responded to the housing shortage of the Great Depression by beginning a massive public housing effort, with all of the new housing racially segregated, and almost all of it only for white people.[81] Richard Rothstein convincingly argues that the New Deal and the public housing projects that continued into the post-war period are the principal cause of segregated neighborhoods in the United States.[82] And the Social Security system, perhaps Roosevelt's greatest legislative achievement, excluded domestic workers and farm workers, thus excluding a substantial part of the Black American work force.[83]

In the late 1940s and early 1950s, President Truman encouraged employers to engage in voluntary affirmative action, as did President Eisenhower in the mid-to late 1950s.[84] President Kennedy expanded those efforts through the President's Committee On Equal Employment Opportunity (PCEEO).[85] In 1961, President Kennedy signed Executive Order 10925, which required government contractors to develop "affirmative action" plans,[86] which at that point meant voluntary – not compulsory – non-discrimination and proportional hiring by large employers.[87] The Executive Order was revised and reissued by President Johnson[88] and remains in effect today, as does a common theme among political and corporate leaders of urging voluntary efforts to increase the number of minority employees, sometimes with proportional goals and sometimes replace.[89]

---

80 Moreno, ibid., at 530.

81 Richard Rothstein, *The Color of Law: A Forgotten History of How Our Government Segregated America* (New York: Liveright, 2017) at 18–21 and passim.

82 Ibid.

83 Whether the exclusion was a political compromise required to win the support of Southern legislators is a contested question. See, Larry Dewitt, "The Decision to Exclude Agricultural and Domestic Workers from the 1935 Social Security Act," *Social Security Bulletin* 70, no. 4 (2010).

84 Exec. Order No. 9980, 3 C.F.R. (1948); Dean J. Kotlowski, "Richard Nixon and the Origins of Affirmative Action," *The Historian* 60, no. 3 (1998): 525; Harry S. Truman, "Special Message to the Congress on Civil Rights," (speech, Washington D.C., February 2, 1948), accessed February 15, 2018. https://www.trumanlibrary.org/public papers/index.php?pid=1380&st=&st1=.

85 Exec. Order. No. 10925, 26 FR 1977 (1961).

86 Ibid.

87 *See United Steelworkers* 443 U.S. at 199–200.

88 Exec. Order. No. 11246, 30 FR 12319 (1965).

89 Oppenheimer, "The Disappearance of Voluntary Affirmative Action from the U.S. Workplace," 44.

The turning point in prohibiting employment discrimination under U.S. law came in 1964 with the passage of the 1964 Civil Rights Act. Title VII of the Act prohibits private and public employers from discriminating based on race, sex, national origin, color, or religion. In the debate over the 1964 Civil Rights Act, one of the critical questions was what impact it would have on voluntary affirmative action by private and public employers. In the debates over the wording of the statute, some had demanded language that prohibited the use of racial preferences.[90] The opponents of the Act complained that without such a provision employers, in order to comply with the non-discrimination mandate, would be required to engage in quota hiring.[91] At least some of the proponents insisted that quota hiring would be prohibited because the Act required non-discrimination for all, embracing a viewpoint of formal equality.[92] Others wanted to include mandatory affirmative action preferences as an explicit part of the remedies available under the Act, insisting on a system of substantive equality.[93] The compromise was language that provided that racial preferences would be neither required nor prohibited.[94] Employers were thus permitted, but not required, to engage in race or gender based numerical proportional hiring.[95]

As affirmative action policies became increasingly controversial and politicized, numerous court cases were brought by white workers or job applicants complaining about affirmative action programs and describing them as "reverse discrimination."[96] In the 1970s and 1980s, a series of Supreme Court decisions distinguished affirmative action by private employers from affirmative action by public employers.[97] In those cases in which the employer was either a state or local governmental entity, the Court applied the

90 Michael K. Brown, Martin Carnoy, Elliott Currie, Troy Duster, David B. Oppenheimer, Marjorie M. Shultz and David Wellman, *Whitewashing Race: The Myth of a Color-Blind Society* (Berkeley: University of California Press, 2003), 170–172.

91 Ibid.; William A. Garrison and Andre Modigliani, "The changing culture of affirmative action," *Equal employment opportunity: labor market discrimination and public policy*, ed. Paul Burstein (New York: Aldine Transaction, 1994), 373.

92 Ibid.

93 Oppenheimer, "Dr. King's Dream of Affirmative Action," 61.

94 *See United Steelworkers*, 443 U.S. at 197 (Brennan, J., delivering the opinion of the Court); Oppenheimer, "The Disappearance of Voluntary Affirmative Action from the U.S. Workplace," 40.

95 Brown, *Whitewashing Race*, 172; *United Steelworkers*, 443 U.S. at 197.

96 *United Steelworkers*, 443 U.S. at 208–209; *see generally Johnson v. Transportation Agency*, 480 U.S. 616 (1987); *City of Richmond v. J.A. Croson Co.*, 488 U.S. 469 (1989); *Adarand Constructors, Inc. v. Pena*, 115 S. Ct. 2097 (1995).

97 *See e.g., McDonald v. Santa Fe Trail Transp.*, 427 U.S. 273 (1976).

14th Amendment's Equal Protection Clause, with a formal equality reading, and limited affirmative action to cases in which it was remedial, based on the employer having previously engaged in illegal discrimination.[98]

In the private sector, the case law was very different. In the two cases in which an affirmative action employment program was challenged under the 1964 Civil Rights Act, the Court upheld the programs, although not without limitations. In *United Steelworkers of America v. Weber*,[99] a white worker challenged an employer's apprenticeship training program that had been negotiated with the steelworkers' union, because it required that half of the employees going into the apprenticeship program be Black. If seniority alone had governed admission to the program, the white employee would have been admitted. The Supreme Court affirmed the racial quotas, holding that private employers could voluntarily adopt racial preferences for the purpose of addressing manifest imbalances in the workplace as long as they were intended to create – rather than maintain – a racial balance, and did not upset established employment rights. The Weber holding was reaffirmed in *Johnson v. Transportation Agency of Santa Clara County.*[100] This case was brought against a public employer but relied only on Title VII, not on a Constitutional claim. The Court held that the use of gender for affirmative action purposes was also permissible, subject to the limitations articulated in *Weber*.

In both *Weber* and *Johnson*, the programs concerned promotions, and the employers did not eliminate all promotions for whites or men. In each instance, the Court held that when the employer has a manifest imbalance in its workforce that disadvantages a traditionally marginalized group, the employer may engage in preferences or quotas for at least a limited time in order to correct the imbalance.[101] Both decisions thus complied with, but did not cite or rely on, the position of the international conventions that temporary affirmative action does not violate the anti-discrimination principle, but that permanent quotas would.

Beginning in the 1980s, a shift occurred away from voluntary affirmative action policies and toward diversity management policies.[102] When Ronald Reagan sought the presidency in 1980, he ran on an anti-affirmative

---

98 *See generally Croson Co.*, 488 U.S.; *Adarand Constructors, Inc.*, 115 S. Ct.

99 *United Steelworkers*, 443 U.S. at 197–200.

100 *Johnson* 480 U.S. at 626–628.

101 *See United Steelworkers*, 443 U.S. at 208–209; *see also, Johnson*, 480 U.S. at 626–628.

102 Erin Kelly and Frank Dobbin, "How affirmative action became diversity management: Employer response to antidiscrimination law, 1961 to 1996," *American Behavioral Scientist* 41, no. 7 (1998): 960–984; Oppenheimer, "The Disappearance of Voluntary Affirmative Action from the U.S. Workplace," 42–47.

action platform, encouraging the growth of resistance to affirmative action programs.[103] Over the next decade, private employers seeing the writing on the walls began to abandon their voluntary affirmative action programs in favor of what they called "diversity management."[104] Outside of the area of government contracting, where the Executive Order still requires some level of affirmative action, most large employers now have diversity programs but not affirmative action programs.[105] While voluntary affirmative action programs by private employers remains lawful under the cases decided by the Supreme Court, they are now uncommon.[106]

Diversity programs rarely include quotas, goals, or timetables, and are more likely to emphasize policies like sensitivity training, mentoring, and affinity groups.[107] The most popular diversity policies are diversity training and diversity evaluations, both of which focus on alerting managers to their own, often implicit, bias.[108] Diversity training does this by having people attend meetings where they are taught about bias and the harm it causes, while diversity evaluations are programs where a person's bias or lack thereof is noted in regular performance evaluations.[109] Unfortunately, both diversity training and diversity

---

103 Kelly and Dobbin, "How affirmative action became diversity management: Employer response to antidiscrimination law, 1961 to 1996," 966; Oppenheimer, "The Disappearance of Voluntary Affirmative Action from the U.S. Workplace," 39.

104 Kelly and Dobbin, "How affirmative action became diversity management: Employer response to antidiscrimination law, 1961 to 1996," 970; Oppenheimer, "The Disappearance of Voluntary Affirmative Action from the U.S. Workplace," 40.

105 Kelly and Dobbin, "How affirmative action became diversity management: Employer response to antidiscrimination law, 1961 to 1996," 971; Oppenheimer, "The Disappearance of Voluntary Affirmative Action from the U.S. Workplace," 41.

106 Oppenheimer, "The Disappearance of Voluntary Affirmative Action from the U.S. Workplace," 41.

107 Jesse E. Olsen and Luis L. Martins, "Understanding organizational diversity management programs: A theoretical framework and directions for future research," *Journal of Organizational Behavior* 33, no. 8 (2012): 1177; Oppenheimer, "The Disappearance of Voluntary Affirmative Action from the U.S. Workplace," 46–47; *see also*, Alexandra Kalev, Erin Kelly, and Frank Dobbin, "Best Practices or Best Guesses? Assessing the Efficacy of Corporate Affirmative Action and Diversity Policies," *American Sociological Review* 71, (2006): 610–612.

108 Oppenheimer, "The Disappearance of Voluntary Affirmative Action from the U.S. Workplace," 46, box 1; *see also*, Kalev, Kelly, and Dobbin, "Best Practices or Best Guesses? Assessing the Efficacy of Corporate Affirmative Action and Diversity Policies," 610–612.

109 Olsen and Martins, "Understanding organizational diversity," 1177; Oppenheimer, "The Disappearance of Voluntary Affirmative Action from the U.S. Workplace," 46; *see also*, Kalev, Kelly, and Dobbin, "Best Practices or Best Guesses? Assessing the Efficacy of Corporate Affirmative Action and Diversity Policies," 593–594.

evaluations were found to be amongst the least effective forms of promoting diversity as they often caused a backlash amongst those subjected to them unless there were mechanisms in place to hold them accountable.[110] Thus, the most popular policies are apparently also the least effective.[111] Generally, diversity policies have done far less to encourage the hiring and promotion of women and minorities than the affirmative action programs that preceded them.[112]

1.3 *Positive Measures in Employment in Canada*

In the mid-1970s, Canada's major unions (i.e., Canadian Labor Congress, Canadian Union of Public Employees, the Public Service Alliance of Canada) began to develop Affirmative Action programs in order to address workplace inequality.[113] In 1978, the federal government began a voluntary Affirmative Action program targeting the private sector.[114]

In 1982, Parliament adopted the Canadian Charter of Rights and Freedoms.[115] Section 15(1) provides: "Every individual is equal before and under the law and has the right to the equal protection and equal benefit of the law without discrimination and, in particular, without discrimination based on race, national or ethnic origin, colour, religion, sex, age or mental or physical disability."[116] Section 15(2) covers affirmative action programs[117] and provides that "[s]ubsection (1) does not preclude any law, program or activity that has

110 Olsen and Martins, "Understanding organizational diversity," 1177; Oppenheimer, "The Disappearance of Voluntary Affirmative Action from the U.S. Workplace," 46; *see also*, Kalev, Kelly, and Dobbin, "Best Practices or Best Guesses? Assessing the Efficacy of Corporate Affirmative Action and Diversity Policies," 610–612.

111 Olsen and Martins, "Understanding organizational diversity," 1177; Oppenheimer, "The Disappearance of Voluntary Affirmative Action from the U.S. Workplace," 46; *see also*, Kalev, Kelly, and Dobbin, "Best Practices or Best Guesses? Assessing the Efficacy of Corporate Affirmative Action and Diversity Policies," 610–612.

112 Olsen and Martins, "Understanding organizational diversity," 1182; Oppenheimer, "The Disappearance of Voluntary Affirmative Action from the U.S. Workplace," 46–47; *see also*, Kalev, Kelly, and Dobbin, "Best Practices or Best Guesses? Assessing the Efficacy of Corporate Affirmative Action and Diversity Policies," 610–612.

113 "A Brief History of Employment Equity in Canada," *Public Service Alliance of Canada.com*. February 2, 2017, accessed October 29, 2017. http://psacunion.ca/employment-equity-tool-kit-psac-members#history.

114 Ibid.

115 Ibid.

116 Canadian Charter of Rights and Freedoms, Part I of the Constitution Act, 1982, *being* Schedule B to the Canada Act, 1982, c 11 (UK). Accessed October 29. 2017. http://laws-lois.justice.gc.ca/eng/Const/page-15.html.

117 Ibid.

as its object the amelioration of conditions of disadvantaged individuals or groups including those that are disadvantaged because of race, national or ethnic origin, colour, religion, sex, age or mental or physical disability."[118]

In 1983, the federal government introduced the Federal Affirmative Action Program designed to increase the "representation of women, Aboriginal Persons and persons with disabilities in the federal public sector."[119] Also in 1983, the Royal Commission on Equality in Employment was established "to explore ways of 'promoting equality in employment' ... for women, Aboriginal peoples, persons with disabilities, and visible minority persons."[120]

In 1984, the Royal Commission released its "Equality in Employment" Report (also known as the "Abella Report").[121] The author, Rosalie Silberman Abella, is regarded as responsible for creating the concept of Canadian "employment equity."[122] (Abella was subsequently appointed to the Canadian Supreme Court in 2004.)[123] The Commission introduced the phrase employment equity "to describe programs of positive remedy for discrimination in the Canadian workplace."[124] The Commission concluded that voluntary measures are insufficient in responding to the pervasiveness of systemic discrimination in Canadian workplaces and therefore recommended new legislation requiring that all federally regulated employers implement employment equity.[125] Thus, the employers and unions would be expected, where necessary, to adjust "recruitment and hiring practices; promotion practices; equal pay for work of equal value; pension and benefit plans; reasonable accommodation and workplace accessibility; occupational testing and evaluation; occupational qualifications and requirements; parental leave provisions; and opportunities for education and training leaves."[126] The Report states that the goal is to expand "employment opportunities of qualified individuals in designated groups."[127]

118 Ibid.

119 "A Brief History of Employment Equity in Canada."

120 Ibid.

121 Ibid.

122 "The Honourable Rosalie Silberman Abella," *Supreme Court of Canada*. October 2, 2017, accessed October 29, 2017. https://www.scc-csc.ca/judges-juges/bio-eng.aspx?id=rosalie-silberman-abella.

123 Ibid.

124 Commission on Equality in Employment, *Equality in Employment: A Royal Commission*, Ottawa: Minister of Supply and Services Canada, 1984, http://crrf-fcrr.com/images/stories/Equality_in_Employment.pdf (accessed October 29, 2017): 6.

125 Ibid.

126 Ibid. at 6–7.

127 Ibid. at 6.

According to the 1984 Report, after reviewing the U.S. affirmative action approach the Commission confirmed that legislated and enforceable requirements are pivotal to the success of affirmative action programs.[128] Among the Commission's conclusions, the enforcement of employment equity requires an independent, sufficiently funded agency with a qualified staff familiar with labour relations, employment systems, and human rights issues.[129] The agency must maintain ongoing consultative relationships with national and regional businesses, labour organizations, and other designated groups in the development of employment equity guidelines.[130] The term employment equity was meant to distinguish the Canadian policy from popular misconceptions about U.S. affirmative action and, especially, from the notion that affirmative action necessarily meant employment quotas.[131] Abella's policy recommendations did not, at the initial stage, impose quotas.[132] But she did note in her Report, "ultimately it matters little whether in Canada we call this process employment equity or affirmative action, so long as we understand that what we mean by both terms are employment practices designed to eliminate discriminatory barriers and to provide in a meaningful way equitable opportunities in employment."[133]

The Report states that without legislation mandating all employers to implement employment equity, the federal government should encourage employment equity in the private sector through contract compliance,[134] by which "government will agree to purchase goods and services only from businesses that agree to implement employment equity and to abide by other provisions negotiated to reflect local needs, such as the provision of training, transportation, or accommodation in northern or remote areas."[135]

In addition, the Commission recommended a National Childcare Act ensuring consistent standards, taking into account both urban and rural needs, and accommodating for the special needs of children who are native, members of minority groups, or disabled.[136] And until a universal system is available,

128 Ibid. at 6–7.

129 Ibid.

130 Ibid.

131 Anna M. Timpson, *Driven Apart: Women's Employment Equality and Child Care in Canadian Public Policy* (Vancouver: UBC Press, 2002), 118.

132 Ibid. at 119.

133 Ibid. at 118.

134 Commission on Equality in Employment, *Equality in Employment: A Royal Commission*, Ottawa: Minister of Supply and Services Canada, 1984, http://crrf-fcrr.com/images/stories/Equality_in_Employment.pdf (accessed October 29, 2017): 7.

135 Ibid.

136 Ibid.

the Commission urged childcare be made available at least for children whose parents are unable to care for them full-time and for children with disability-based special needs.[137] "Ideally, a childcare system should be publicly funded, of acceptable quality, universally accessible though not compulsory, and available to children from birth at least until the age at which they are legally permitted to remain home unattended by an adult."[138] Anna Timpson argues that childcare was integral to the process of promoting gender equality.[139] One of the laws' anticipated effects was to allow and encourage women to relinquish child care responsibilities in order to allow them to work outside the home.[140] Abella was concerned that workplace child care could tether parents, particularly mothers, to unsatisfactory jobs.[141]

In 1985, "visible minorities" were added to the federal Affirmative Action program.[142] Visible minorities are defined in the Employment Equity Act "as persons, other than Aboriginal peoples, who are non-Caucasian in race or non-white in colour."[143] Categories within the visible minority umbrella include "South Asian, Chinese, Black, Filipino, Latin American, Arab, Southeast Asian, West Asian, Korean, Japanese, Visible minority, n.i.e. (not included elsewhere), [and] Multiple visible minorities ..."[144] Also in 1985, Section 15 (affirmative action programs) of the Charter of Rights and Freedoms came into effect.[145]

In 1986, the federal Employment Equity Act was passed.[146] Section 2 describes the purpose of the act as being,[147] to achieve equality in employment opportunities and benefits in the workplace on grounds other than merit, as a means to correct the injustices dealt to women, aboriginal peoples, persons with disabilities, and members of visible minorities through special measures and the accommodation of differences.[148] Section 5 establishes that it is the

---

137 Ibid.

138 Ibid.

139 Timpson, *Driven Apart*, 146.

140 Ibid. at 140.

141 Ibid. at 147.

142 "A Brief History of Employment Equity in Canada."

143 "Visible Minority and Population Group Reference Guide, National Household Survey, 2011," *Statistics Canada*. December 31, 2015, accessed October 29, 2017. http://www12.statcan.gc.ca/nhs-enm/2011/ref/guides/99-010-x/99-010-x2011009-eng.cfm.

144 Ibid.

145 "A Brief History of Employment Equity in Canada."

146 Ibid.

147 Ibid.

148 Senate and House of Commons of Canada. *Employment Equity Act S.C., 1995, c. 44*. Ottowa: Justice Laws Website, 2012, accessed October 29, 2017. http://laws-lois.justice.gc.ca/eng/acts/e-5.401/page-1.html.

employers' duty to[149] implement employment equity programs designed to identify and eliminate the employment barriers faced by protected groups that are a result of illegal systemic discrimination.[150] This is to be done through positive measures and reasonable accommodations such that the protected groups will have proportional representation.[151] Section 6 establishes that employers are not required to[152] take measures that would cause them undue hardship, or force them to hire or promote unqualified people.[153] For the public sector, Section 6 also establishes that employers do not have to violate the Public Service Employment Act requirement that hiring or promotion should be based on merit or to create new positions in its workforce.[154]

In the 1987 case *CN v. Canada (Canadian Human Rights Commission)*, the Supreme Court of Canada unanimously reversed a Federal Court of Appeals decision and reinstated a Tribal Order requiring the Canadian National Railway to hire one woman for every four entries into its unskilled, blue-collar labor force.[155] As discussed in the Introduction to this work, the Court stated:

> [a]n employment equity program, such as the one in the present case, is designed to break a continuing cycle of systemic discrimination. The goal is not to compensate past victims or even to provide new opportunities for specific individuals who have been unfairly refused jobs or promotion in the past. Rather, an employment equity program is an attempt to ensure that future applicants and workers from the affected group will not face the same insidious barriers that blocked their forebears. In any employment equity program, there simply cannot be a radical dissociation of 'remedy' and 'prevention' for there is no prevention without some form of remedy.[156]

Thus, the purpose of Canada's affirmative action programs is to create a new and more equitable status quo, rather than to only rectify past injustices.

In the late 1980s and 1990s, the expansion of affirmative action continued apace. In 1988, the National Employment Equity Network was created with the goal of lobbying the federal government to increase the effectiveness of the

149 Ibid.
150 Ibid.
151 Ibid.
152 Ibid.
153 Ibid.
154 Ibid.
155 *CN v. Canada* at 1131.
156 Ibid. at 1116.

employment equity program.[157] In 1993, the Ontario Employment Equity Act was passed, extending the mandates of the federal employment equity program to provincially regulated public and private sector workplaces.[158] In 1996, the federal government, the assembly of Manitoba Chiefs, and the Canadian Human Rights Commission reached settlement agreements providing for measures to increase Aboriginal representation and retention in the federal public service.[159]

In 2001, Quebec enacted employment equity legislation by implementing the Act Representing Equal Access to Employment in Public Bodies (respecting equal access to employment in public bodies) and amending the Quebec Charter of Human Rights and Freedoms.[160] Under "[d]ivision 1 – object and scope,"[161] section 1 articulates that:

> [t]his Act establishes a special framework to provide equal access to employment in order to remedy the situation experienced by persons belonging to certain groups discriminated against in employment, namely women, handicapped persons within the meaning of the Act to secure handicapped persons in the exercise of their rights with a view to achieving social, school and workplace integration (chapter E-20.1), aboriginal peoples, persons who are members of visible minorities because of their race or the colour of their skin and persons whose mother tongue is neither French nor English and who belong to a group other than the aboriginal peoples group or the visible minorities group.[162]

In the late 2000s, there were further expansions to Canada's affirmative action programs. In 2006, the Public Service Employment Act was implemented, regarding employment equity in the federal public service's staffing process.[163] In 2007, the Senate Standing Committee on Human Rights produced its first report ("Employment Equity in the Federal Public Service – Not There Yet"), finding that not enough progress has been made in achieving employment equity

157 "A Brief History of Employment Equity in Canada."
158 Ibid.
159 Ibid.
160 Ibid.
161 National Assembly. *Act Respecting Equal Access to Employment in Public Bodies*, A-2.01. (Quebec: Legis Quebec, 2001), accessed October 29, 2017. http://legisquebec.gouv.qc.ca/en/ShowDoc/cs/A-2.01.
162 Ibid.
163 "A Brief History of Employment Equity in Canada."

in the public sector.[164] In 2010, the Senate Standing Committee on Human Rights released its second report ("Reflecting the Changing Face of Canada: Employment Equity in the Federal Public Service"), presenting an even more critical view of the failure to fully implement employment equity programs.[165] In conclusion, Canada has adopted a far-reaching legal requirement of using positive action to reduce substantive inequality.

1.4 *Positive Measures in Employment in India*

Pre-colonial India was governed through a compartmentalized hierarchy, or caste system, in which lower caste Indians, including those in the lowest caste group formerly known as the "Harijans" or "Dalits," (or the now disfavored term "untouchables,") were disadvantaged in every area of life.[166]

During the British Colonial period in India, British rulers largely embraced the traditional caste system as a mechanism of control. While Colonial law did not formally recognize caste order, it recognized autonomy of the castes. For instance, courts tended not to interfere with the "disciplinary powers of castes against violators of received etiquette of inter-caste relations."[167] The British applied separate bodies of law according to religious affiliation of Indian parties in matters of family, property, and religion, but otherwise instituted a general law applicable to all. Marc Galanter explains that "the law did not provide the higher castes with an instrument for aggressively suppressing their inferiors (as, e.g., Jim Crow laws did in post-Reconstruction southern U.S.), but the law provided another resource which high castes could use to protect their claims to precedence."[168] This occurred because the general law established only formal equality before the law, which in practice favored the higher castes as they were the only ones with the economic, legal, and educational resources needed to take advantage of the opportunities the law provided.[169]

Anti-caste movements beginning in the mid-1800s supported some forms of preferential treatment for untouchable castes.[170] Most reform movements

164 Ibid.

165 Ibid.

166 Ashwini Deshpande, *Affirmative Action in India* (Oxford: Oxford University Press, 2013), 11–12.

167 Marc Galanter, *Competing Equalities: Law and the Backward Classes in India* (Berkeley: University of California Press, 1984), 19–20.

168 Ibid. at 21.

169 Ibid.

170 Deshpande, *Affirmative Action in India*, 45–46; *see also*, "Meritorious X, XII Students Honoured by BSP."; "Rajarshi Shahu Chhatrapati of Kolhapur, a Reformer Ahead of His Time."; "Life History of Shahu Chhatrapati."

were organized by the Indian people, with an initial focus on allowing a process of upgrading caste status. Eventually reformers turned toward seeking political representation, government jobs, and scholarships.[171]

Quotas were introduced as part of the colonial policy of permitting various groups to have a voice within the limited self-government permitted under colonial rule. By independence, India had a history of reservations defined by caste for civil service positions and other benefits, the first of which was Chhatrapati Shahu the Maharaja of Kolhapur's 50% reservations for "untouchables" in 1902, which was rolled back by his successors upon his death in 1922.[172] However, starting in the mid 1910s there was a growing movement for affirmative action in India to combat Brahmin dominance over Indian society at the time, which culminated in a nationwide push from anti-Brahmin political parties for reservations for all non-Brahmin castes in both education and state services.[173] Galanter explains that "By stressing the philosophical and tolerant aspects of Hinduism over the ritual and confining, and by advocating a more scientific and rational approach to social change, Indian leaders helped to make untouchability and caste hierarchy seem not only unjust, but also backward and premodern."[174]

Upon gaining its independence, India wrote affirmative action reservations into its 1948 Constitution. These policies reserved places in public employment and admission to public universities for the lower castes and for non-Hindus based on a formula intended to provide equal opportunity both in law and in fact.[175] A principal architect of the constitution, Dr. Bhimrao Ramji Ambedkar, had been supporting and arguing for reserved political representation, government jobs, and educational opportunities for lower caste Indians for decades.[176]

---

171 Galanter, *Competing Equalities: Law and the Backward Classes in India*, 23–24; P.S. Krishnan and Vasanti Devi, *A Crusade for Social Justice, Bending Governance towards the Deprived* (Chennai: South Vision Books, 2017), 169.

172 Deshpande, *Affirmative Action in India*, 49–53; Galanter, *Competing Equalities: Law and the Backward Classes in India*, 27; "Life History of Shahu Chhatrapati."

173 Galanter, *Competing Equalities: Law and the Backward Classes in India*, 27.

174 Sunita Parikh, *The Politics of Preference: Democratic Institutions and Affirmative Action in the United States and India* (Ann Arbor: University of Michigan Press, 1997), 78.

175 Deshpande, *Affirmative Action in India*, 54–55.

176 Galanter, *Competing Equalities: Law and the Backward Classes in India*, 30, 39 (though Dr. Bhimrao Ramji Ambedkar was quickly dissatisfied with the early results of the constitution).

India Const. art. 15 provides, in its entirety, as follows:

> *Prohibition of discrimination on grounds of religion, race, caste, sex, or place of birth.* The State shall not discriminate against any citizen on grounds only of religion, race, caste, sex, place of birth or any of them. No citizen shall, on grounds only of religion, race, caste, sex, place of birth or any of them, be subject to any disability, liability, restriction, or condition with regard to: (a) access to shops, public restaurants, hotels and places of public entertainment; or (b) the use of wells, tanks, bathing ghats, roads and places of public resort maintained wholly or partly out of State funds or dedicated to the use of the general public. Nothing in this article shall prevent the State from making any special provision for women and children. Nothing in this article or in clause (2) of article 29 shall prevent the State from making any special provision for the advancement of any socially and educationally backward classes of citizens or for the Scheduled Castes and the Scheduled Tribes. Nothing in this article or in sub-clause (g) of clause (1) of article 19 shall prevent the state from making any special provision, by law, for the advancement of any socially and educationally backward classes of citizens or for the Scheduled Castes or the Scheduled Tribes in so far as such special provisions relate to their admission to educational institutions including private educational institutions, whether aided or unaided by the state, other than the minority education institutions referred to in clause (1) of article 30.[177]

As can be seen, Article 15 seeks to address numerous forms of inequality throughout Indian society via prohibiting public or private discrimination against Backwards Classes or Scheduled Classes and Tribes.[178] Recently Article 15 was amended to also allow the government to "provide for the advancement of "economically weaker sections."[179]

The present reservation program building on Article 15 divides the Indian population into four broad groups:[180]

---

177 India Const. art. 15.

178 Ibid.

179 Ministry of Social Justice and Empowerment, *The Constitution (One Hundred and Twenty Fourth Amendment) Bill, 2019.* New Delhi: PRS Legislative Research, 2019. Accessed February 22, 2019. https://www.prsindia.org/billtrack/constitution-one-hundred-and-twenty-fourth-amendment-bill-2019.

180 Deshpande, *Affirmative Action in India*, 18.

1. Scheduled Castes (SC) (ex-untouchable jatis or 'Dalit'), about eighteen percent of the population;
2. Scheduled Tribes (ST), about eight percent of the population;
3. Other Backward Classes (OBC) (heterogeneous collection of Hindu low castes, some non-Hindu communities, and some tribes which are not included in Scheduled Tribes), about forty-three percent of rural population and thirty-nine percent of urban population. Many of these subcastes are Shudra subcastes.[181] Quotas for this group are the most litigated.[182]
4. Residual (everyone else) (the data do not isolate the upper castes).

This thus enables much of the population of India to benefit from affirmative action quotas by classifying a large swath of the population as disadvantaged.

Constitution of India Article 16 provides a broad constitutional basis for both anti-discrimination and affirmative action, as follows:[183]

> (1) There shall be equality of opportunity for all citizens in matters relating to employment or appointment to any office under the State.
> (2) No citizen shall, on grounds only of religion, race, caste, sex, descent, place of birth, residence or any of them, be ineligible for, or discriminated against in respect of, any employment or office under the State.
> (3) [omitted]
> (4) Nothing in this article shall prevent the State from making any provision for the reservation of appointments or posts in favour of any backward class of citizens which, in the opinion of the State, is not adequately represented in the services under the State.

In *M.R. Balaji v. State of Mysore*,[184] the Supreme Court of India had to synthesize Articles 16(1) and (2) of the Constitution (prohibiting discrimination in public employment on grounds of caste) with Article 16(4) (enabling reservations for "backward classes"[185]). The mis-alignment raised problems for caste-based affirmative action, as *exclusio unius* would imply that caste and class

181 Kevin D. Brown and Vinay Sitapati, "Lessons Learned from Comparing the Application of Constitutional Law and Federal Anti-Discrimination Law to African-Americans in the U.S. and Dalits in India in the Context of Higher Education," *Harvard Blackletter Law Journal* 24 (2008): 17.

182 Deshpande, *Affirmative Action in India*, 126–127.

183 INDIA CONST. art. 16.

184 *M.R. Balaji v. State of Mysore*, AIR 1963 SC 649.

185 Gautam Bhatia, "Caste and the Law," *India Law ejournal* 15, no. 12 (2019): 4–5. Accessed February 22, 2019. https://papers.ssrn.com/sol3/papers.cfm?abstract_id=3325812.

are separate categories.[186] The court resolved the problem by holding that although there was a distinction between "caste" and "class," caste could be a useful proxy for determining which classes were backward.[187] Accordingly, while affirmative action could not be done by caste alone, the legislature could identify a set of castes, verify that they were "backwards", and create appropriate affirmative action programs.[188] Recently, Article 16 was amended to create a 10% reservation in government employment for "economically weaker sections," a categorization based on family income rather than on caste status.[189]

Balaji, in turn, served as the basis for the famous *Sawhney v. Union of India* (1993)[190] decision, where the Indian Supreme Court held that reservations in favor of the "backward classes" are permissible under the Indian Constitution; that reservations should be made based on caste membership, which is equated with social class; that reservations should generally be limited to 50%; that classification should be based on degrees of social backwardness; that wealthy members of a backward class (the "creamy layer") should be excluded from reservations; that reservations should be limited to appointments, and should not be used for promotions; and that the Government should appoint a permanent body to determine lists of backward classes.[191]

In *Meera Kanwaria v. Sunita and Others* (2006),[192] a woman from the Rajput caste (a higher caste) married a man from a scheduled caste, and thereafter ran for public office (the municipal counsel), seeking a seat reserved for members of the scheduled castes. (Reservations and parity democracy will be discussed infra, at p. 86.) Although by marrying a member of a scheduled caste she had taken on his social status, the Indian Supreme Court held that she was ineligible for the reserved seat because the reservation was intended to compensate for disadvantages she had not suffered having been born in a "forward caste."

In *Thakur v. Union of India* (2007),[193] The Indian Supreme Court, sitting as a two-justice bench, re-affirmed that a 50 percent reservation of jobs and higher education placements for "socially and educationally backward classes

186 Ibid.

187 Ibid.

188 Ibid.

189 Ministry of Social Justice and Empowerment, *The Constitution (One Hundred and Twenty Fourth Amendment) Bill, 2019*. New Delhi: PRS Legislative Research, 2019. Accessed February 22, 2019. https://www.prsindia.org/billtrack/constitution-one-hundred-and-twenty-fourth-amendment-bill-2019.

190 Ibid; *Sawhney v. Union of India*, AIR 1993 SC 477.

191 Bhatia, "Caste and the Law," 5; *Sawhney* AIR 1993 SC 477.

192 *Meera Kanwaria v. Sunita and Others*, AIR 2006 SC 597.

193 *Thakur v. Union of India*, (2007) 4 SCC 361.

of society" is reasonable, and that the "creamy layer" should be excluded from those eligible for reservations.[194] In *Thakur v. Union of India and Others*, five justices affirmed the two-justice bench.[195] The justices called for a shift from strict caste-based affirmative action to a more flexible approach in determining social backwardness, as well as establishing indicators of who qualified for the "creamy layer."[196]

Following the 1990 extension of the reservations to include "backward classes" as well as scheduled castes and tribes, various communities have lobbied to be included as "backward" in order to receive reservations for their members in government jobs.[197] For two examples, the Meena and the Gujjar communities in Rajasthan are fighting to be deemed backward, although neither of them were originally listed as such.[198] A third example has been especially controversial. The Patels, although dominant in Gujarat, where many of their members are prominent, successful, and wealthy beyond their share of 15% of the State's population, are also lobbying for "backward" status.[199] In August 2015, eight people were killed in demonstrations led by the Patel community, demanding quotas in educational institutions and government jobs.[200]

A form of reservations has recently been extended to persons with disabilities, through a policy[201] requiring government authorities to provide incentives to public and private employers to ensure that at least five percent of their workforce is composed of persons with disabilities.[202]

Article 15(3) of the Indian Constitution allows the state to make special provisions for women in employment.[203] In *Government of Andhra Pradesh v. P.B Vijay Kumar*,[204] the Indian Supreme Court held that reservation of posts for women, or special preferences given to them, were constitutionally valid

---

194 Ibid.

195 *Thakur v. Union of India and Others*, (2008) 6 SCC 1.

196 Ibid.

197 Sujit Raman, "Caste in Stone: Consequences of India's Affirmative Action Policies," *Harvard International Review* 21, no. 4 (1999): 30–34.

198 Ibid.

199 *See* "Why India news a new debate on caste quota," *BBC News*. August 29, 2015, accessed February 2019. http://www.bbc.com/news/world-asia-india-34082770.

200 *See* Ibid.

201 Ministry of Law and Justice. The Rights of Persons with Disabilities Act, 2016. New Delhi: Gazette of India (Extra-Ordinary). Accessed Feb. 24, 2018. Chapter VI Section 35. http://www.upfcindia.com/documents/rpwd_101017.pdf.

202 Ibid.

203 INDIA CONST. art. 15.

204 *Govt. of A.P v. P.B Vijayakumar* 1995 4 SCC 520.

under Article 15(3). "Article 15(3) recognizes the fact that the women in India have been socially and economically [disadvantaged] for centuries and, as the result thereof, they cannot fully participate in the socio-economic activities of the nation on a footing of equality."[205] The purpose of Article 15(3) is to eliminate the socio-economic disadvantages of being a woman and to empower women to achieve effective equality between men and women.[206]

In conclusion, India has a long history of using caste-based discrimination to entrench the interests of the upper classes. But as Indian democracy developed, its Constitution and successive governments sought to use positive measures, in the form of reservations, to fight inequality. Determining who precisely should benefit, however, is an ongoing point of contention. Over time, much of the population has come to feel that too many of those who benefit from positive measures are not truly disadvantaged and have demanded that reservations be reduced. But members of groups not included in the reservations policies have demanded that they be expanded. The Indian Supreme Court has sought to rectify this problem by requiring the exclusion of the "creamy layer" from reservation benefits. The adoption of the creamy layer test illustrates that India's underlying rationale for positive measures has somewhat changed. It has shifted from the simple position that all members of the Backwards Classes or Scheduled Classes and Tribes deserve help, to the view that only those suffering actual economic disadvantage deserve positive measures. In the process, the policy has moved from providing support for those of a lower social status, to aiding those of a lower economic status. But it has retained the empirically sound presumption that lower social status usually leads to lower economic status, thus justifying group-based affirmative measures.

1.5 *Positive Measures in Employment in South Africa*

In 1948, the Afrikaner National Party (ANP) of South Africa was elected to power, in an election in which only whites could vote, on a promise to institute a policy of racial apartheid.[207]

During the apartheid period, the South African government enacted legislation based on racial classification starting with the Population Registration Act of 1950, which divided the South African population into three main racial

205 Amrita Mitra, *Affirmative Action for Women in Indian Constitution*, 4. August 15, 2012, accessed November 11, 2018. http://dx.doi.org/10.2139/ssrn.2129663.

206 Ibid.

207 Cornel Verwey and Michael Quayle, "Whiteness, Racism, and Afrikaner Identity in Post-Apartheid South Africa," *African Affairs* 111, no. 445 (2012): 553.

groups: "Whites," "Natives" (Black people), and "Indians and Coloured people" (people of mixed race).[208] Under apartheid, Black people were forcibly removed from their homes if these were situated in neighborhoods designated by law as white residential areas, they received inferior education, and they had their access to the labor market and freedom of movement severely restricted.[209] Black and Coloured persons were denied entry to universities, while the number of Indian students was strictly limited. All non-whites were largely prohibited from working in most job categories.[210] For mixed race South Africans, the Prohibition of Mixed Marriages Act of 1949 (banning "marriage between persons of different races") and the Immorality Act of 1950 (criminalizing "sexual relations with a person of a different race") were particularly devastating.[211]

In 1994, after forty-six years of increasing international isolation, the ANP abandoned their apartheid policies, leading to the country's first multi-racial elections.[212] African National Congress (ANC) leader Nelson Mandela, released after twenty-seven years in prison for his opposition to apartheid, was elected president.[213] In the wake of Mandela's election and the ANC's election as the ruling party, a series of laws were passed to abolish discrimination and establish a system of positive measures to remedy discrimination and promote equality.

In July 1995, the Truth and Reconciliation Commission was established based on the Promotion of the National Unity and Reconciliation Amendment, No Act 34 of 1995 "to help deal with what happened under apartheid."[214]

In December 1996, President Mandela signed the Constitution of the Republic of South Africa into law, replacing the previous interim Constitution.[215] Under section 9 – Equality:

---

208 "Race and ethnicity in South Africa," *South African History*. Accessed March 21, 2018. http://www.sahistory.org.za/article/race-and-ethnicity-south-africa.

209 *See Brink v. Kitshoff* (1996) 4 SA 197 (CC) para 40; David B. Oppenheimer et al. *Comparative Equality & Anti-Discrimination Law*, 2nd ed. (Berkeley: Comparative Equality Press, 2017), 238.

210 "Race and ethnicity in South Africa."

211 Ibid.

212 Nicolas Pons-Vignon and Ward Anseeuw, "Great Expectations: Working Conditions in South Africa since the End of Apartheid," *Journal of Southern African Studies* 35, no. 4 (2009): 883.

213 Christopher J. Lee, "Mourning Mandela," *Transition*, no. 116 (2014): 171.

214 "Welcome to the official Truth and Reconciliation Commission Website," *Truth and Reconciliation Commission*, accessed February 23, 2018. http://www.justice.gov.za/trc/index.html.

215 "The Constitution: The Certification Process," *Constitutional Court of South Africa*, accessed February 23, 2018. https://www.concourt.org.za/index.php/constitution/the-certification-process.

> Everyone is equal before the law and has the right to equal protection and benefit of the law. Equality includes the full and equal enjoyment of all rights and freedoms.... The state may not *unfairly* [*emphasis added*] discriminate directly or indirectly against anyone on one or more grounds, including race, gender, sex, pregnancy, marital status, ethnic or social origin, colour, sexual orientation, age, disability, religion, conscience, belief, culture, language and birth.... National legislation must be enacted to prevent or prohibit unfair discrimination.[216]

Additionally, section 9(2) of the Bill of Rights states that in order "to promote the achievement of equality, legislative and other measures designed to protect or advance persons, or categories of persons, disadvantaged by unfair discrimination may be taken."[217]

In 1998, the Employment Equity Act was passed.[218] Part 1 (definitions, purpose, interpretation and application), section 2 provides:

> [t]he purpose of the Act is to achieve equity in the workplace, by promoting equal opportunity and fair treatment in employment through the elimination of unfair discrimination; and implementing affirmative action measures to redress the disadvantages in employment experienced by designated groups, to ensure their equitable representation in all occupational categories and levels in the workforce.[219]

The Act thus expressly establishes that affirmative action is not merely allowed, but is required in South Africa as part of a larger bid to make a more equal society.

Part 2 (prohibition of unfair discrimination), section 6(1) provides:

> No person may unfairly discriminate, directly or indirectly, against an employee in any employment policy or practice, on one or more grounds including race, gender, pregnancy, marital status, family responsibility,

216 S. Afr. Const., 1996, section 9.

217 Ibid.

218 *See generally*, South African Parliament, *Employment Equity Act 1998*, Cape Town: Government Gazette, 1998. Accessed November 17, 2017. http://www.labour.gov.za/DOL/downloads/legislation/acts/employment-equity/eegazette2015.pdf.

219 Ibid. at 12.

> ethnic or social origin, colour, sexual orientation, age, disability, religion, HIV status, conscience, belief, political opinion, culture, language, and birth.[220]

Endorsing a substantive equality doctrine in favor of formal equality, section 6(2) provides, "[i]t is not unfair discrimination to promote affirmative action consistent with the Act or to prefer or exclude any person on the basis of an inherent job requirement."[221]

Part 3 (affirmative action), section 13 provides:

> Every designated employer must, in order to achieve employment equity, implement affirmative action measures for people from designated groups in terms of this act. (2) A designated employer must: (a) consult with employees as required in section 16; (b) conduct an analysis as required by section 19; (c) prepare an employment equity plan as required by section 20; and (d) report to the Director-General on progress made in the implementation of the plan, as required by section 21.[222]

The Act thereby establishes concrete steps that employers must take as part of South Africa's drive toward workplace equality.

Section 15(1) defines affirmative action measures as those intended to ensure that suitably qualified employees from designated groups have equal employment opportunity and are equitably represented in all occupational categories and levels of the workforce."[223] Such measures include promoting diversity, "making reasonable accommodation for people from designated groups," and "preferential treatment and numerical goals, but exclude quotas."[224] Section 24(1) requires employers to assign at least one senior manager to ensure implementation and monitoring of the employment equity plan.[225] Under section 27(2), "where there are disproportionate income differentials" in an occupational category or level of the workforce, the employer "must take measures to reduce it progressively."[226]

---

220 Ibid. at 14.
221 Ibid.
222 Ibid. at 18.
223 Ibid. at 18, 20.
224 Ibid.
225 Ibid. at 26.
226 Ibid. at 26–28.

In 2004, the Constitutional Court heard the case *Minister of Finance and Another v. Van Heerden*, 2004 (6) SA 121 (CC) regarding preferential pension benefits to members of Parliament from groups that previously faced race-based discrimination and were prohibited from being members of Parliament prior to 1994.[227] The Court upheld the measure as constitutional.[228] Deputy Chief Justice Moseneke clarified Section 9(2) of the Bill of Rights:

> [T]he enquiry is threefold. The first yardstick relates to whether the measure targets persons or categories of persons who have been disadvantaged by unfair discrimination; the second is whether the measure is designed to protect or advance such persons or categories of persons; and the third requirement is whether the measure promotes the achievement of equality.[229]

The Chief Justice also distinguished the South African approach from the U.S.'s "strict judicial scrutiny" under the 14th Amendment, explaining:[230]

> The US anti-discrimination approach regards affirmative action measures as a suspect category which must pass strict judicial scrutiny. The test requires that it be demonstrated that differentiation on the grounds of race is a necessary means to the promotion of a compelling or overriding state interest. A rational relationship between the differentiation and a state interest would be inadequate. Our equality jurisprudence differs substantively from the US approach to equality. Our respective histories, social context and constitutional design differ markedly.[231]

In sum, affirmative action is not only lawful in South Africa; it is required in many employment settings.

---

227 *Minister of Finance and Another v. Van Heerden*, 2004 (6) SA 121 (CC) at para 1–3; Oppenheimer et al., *Comparative Equality & Anti-Discrimination Law*, 238–239.

228 *Van Heerden*, 2004 (6) SA 121 (CC) at para 33; Oppenheimer et al., *Comparative Equality & Anti-Discrimination Law*, 238–239.

229 *Van Heerden*, 2004 (6) SA 121 (CC) at para 37; Oppenheimer et al., *Comparative Equality & Anti-Discrimination Law*, 238–239.

230 *Van Heerden*, 2004 (6) SA 121 (CC) at para 29; Oppenheimer et al., *Comparative Equality & Anti-Discrimination Law*, 239–240.

231 *Van Heerden*, 2004 (6) SA 121 (CC) at para 29; Oppenheimer et al., *Comparative Equality & Anti-Discrimination Law*, 239.

1.6 *Positive Measures in Employment in Brazil*

Brazil was the largest importer of African slaves in the world.[232] As a result, most living Brazilians are descendants of the three racial/ethnic groups who populated Brazil during colonial times – Portuguese colonialists, indigenous people, and African slaves.[233] Although Brazil has high rates of so-called "miscegenation," Brazilian society has a clear racial hierarchy.[234] The racial divide is especially notable in the education, media, and employment sectors.[235] People who identify as white are at the top of the socio-economic hierarchy.[236] Racially-mixed individuals fall just below, while Afro-Brazilians remain at the bottom of the hierarchy.[237] Darker skinned Brazilians are associated with the lower class, have less access to education, and generally hold less prestigious jobs.[238] Whiteness, on the other hand, is correlated with money, higher education, and better employment opportunities.[239] Rafael Guerreiro Osorio writes, "As Brazil has been a very unequal society throughout its history, those at the bottom have always been far below those at the top – the descendents of the European colonisers."[240]

Brazil is a self-described "racial democracy," in which equality is a founding principle of the modern state.[241] As explained by the Brazilian Supreme Court, the Brazilian approach to affirmative action "consistently emphasizes the constitutional principle of equality (isonomia), which mandates compensation for the past discrimination that created current racial inequalities."[242] Abdias

232 Johnson III and Heringer, *Race, Politics, and Education in Brazil*, 1.

233 Stanley R. Bailey, *Legacies of Race Identities, Attitudes, and Policies in Brazil* (Stanford: Stanford University Press, 2009): 1.

234 Martins, Medeiros and Nascimento, "Paving Paradise: the Road from 'Racial Democracy' to Affirmative Action in Brazil," 809.

235 Htun, "From 'Racial Democracy' to Affirmative Action: Changing State Policy on Race in Brazil," 74. https://doi.org/10.1353/lar.2004.0010.

236 Ibid. at 62; Bernardino-Costa and Blackman, "Affirmative Action in Brazil," 374.

237 Htun, "Racial Democracy," 62; Bernardino-Costa and Blackman, "Affirmative Action in Brazil," 374.

238 Htun, "Racial Democracy," 74.

239 Ibid.

240 Rafael Guerreiro Osorio, "The Persistence of Black-White Income Differentials in Brazil," in *Affirmative Action in Plural Societies: International Experiences*, eds. Graham K. Brown, Arnim Langer, and Frances Stewart (New York: Palgrave Macmillan, 2012): 119.

241 George Reid Andrews, "Brazilian Racial Democracy, 1900–90: An American Counterpoint," *Journal of Contemporary History* 31, no. 3 (1996): 483; *See also*, Oppenheimer et al., *Comparative Equality & Anti-Discrimination Law*, 255.

242 Sérgio Da Silva Martins, Carlos Alberto Medeiros and Elisa Larkin Nascimento, "Paving Paradise: the Road from 'Racial Democracy' to Affirmative Action in Brazil," *Journal of Black Studies* 34, no. 6 (2004): 811.

do Nascimento (a former senator and prominent Afro-Brazilian scholar and artist) prefers the term "compensatory action" to affirmative action.[243] Former Supreme Federal Tribunal President Mello believed that in order to implement the constitutional principle of equality, the Brazilian state must pay "'historical debts' owed ... to social minorities, in particular African Brazilians."[244] These debts are born out of the treatment of African Brazilians during the country's past as one of the largest slave trading nations in the world.[245] This past resulted in Brazil having both the largest proportion of the African diaspora as well as a massive disparity in living conditions between those identified as white and those identified as black.[246] Therefore, the Brazilian state had obligated itself to affirmatively prevent racial discrimination.[247]

In October 2018, however, Brazil elected Jair Bolsonaro President.[248] President Bolsonaro is an outspoken opponent of affirmative action. He insists that modern Brazilians owe Afro-Brazilians nothing for the previous injustices they have suffered.[249] He asserts that as Brazil is a mixed-race nation, the concept of race is inapplicable to Brazilians, and so such forms of affirmative action are entirely pointless.[250] He has promised to reduce Brazil's affirmative action programs, though his ability to do so, as of May 2019, is unproven.[251]

---

243 Ibid.

244 Ibid.

245 Ollie A. Johnson III and Rosana Heringer, eds., *Race, Politics, and Education in Brazil* (New York: Palgrave Macmillan., 2015), 1. doi:10.1057/9781137485151.

246 Mala Htun, "From 'Racial Democracy' to Affirmative Action: Changing State Policy on Race in Brazil," *Latin American Research Review* 60, no. 1 (2004): 62; Joaze Bernardino-Costa and Ana E. Blackman, "Affirmative Action in Brazil and Building an Anti-racist University," *Race Ethnicity and Education* 20, no. 3 (2017): 374. http://dx.doi.org/10.1080/13613324.2016.1260228.

247 Christopher Dischino, "Affirmative Action in Brazil: Reverse Discrimination and the Creation of a Constitutionally Protected Color-Line," *University of Miami International and Comparative Law Review* 155 (2014): 177.

248 Ernesto Londoño, and Shasta Darlington, "Jair Bolsonaro Wins Brazil's Presidency, in a Shift to the Far Right," *The New York Times*. October 28, 2018, accessed February 3, 2019. https://www.nytimes.com/2018/10/28/world/americas/jair-bolsonaro-brazil-election.html.

249 Biller, "Bolsonaro Says Black Brazilians Aren't Owed Anything Over Slavery."; Sarah Lempp, "Jair Bolsonaro and Affirmative Action: Political Rupture or Escalation?" Allegra, April 2, 2019, accessed May 15, 2019. http://allegralaboratory.net/jair-bolsonaro-and-affirmative-action-political-rupture-or-escalation/.

250 Lempp, "Jair Bolsonaro and Affirmative Action: Political Rupture or Escalation?"

251 *See* Ciara Nugent, "How Far-Right Populist Jair Bolsonaro Could Transform Brazil," *Time*. October 25, 2018, accessed February 3, 2019. http://time.com/5433379/brazil-bolsonaro-policies/; David Biller, "Bolsonaro Says Black Brazilians Aren't Owed Anything Over Slavery," *Bloomberg.com*. July 31, 2018, accessed February 3, 2019. https://www.bloomberg.

The Brazilian Constitution of 1934 was the first revision to declare "[a]ll are equal under the law. There shall not be any privileges, nor distinctions for reasons of birth, sex, race, personal or family occupation, social class, wealth, religious beliefs, or political ideas."[252] The 1937 and 1946 Constitutions eliminated the 1934 language and declared only that "[a]ll shall be equal in the eyes of the law."[253] Brazil's 1967 Constitution reintroduced the explicit prohibition of racial discrimination by adding the phrase "racial prejudice will be punished by law."[254] And the Constitution of 1988 (the current version) "characterizes equality as an inviolable right; authorizes government action to achieve equality; and establishes racial discrimination as a crime punishable by incarceration, for which bail may not be posted, and to which no statute of limitations applies."[255] It once again establishes that "everyone is equal before the law."[256] Article 3 of the Brazilian Constitution states "the fundamental objectives of the Federative Republic of Brazil are: to build a free, just and solidary society; to guarantee national development; to eradicate poverty and substandard living conditions and to reduce social and regional inequalities; to promote the well-being of all, without prejudice as to origin, race, sex, colour, age and any other forms of discrimination."[257]

In 1985, Brazil returned to democratic rule with the end of a military dictatorship.[258] At that time, social movements launched public education

---

com/news/articles/2018-07-31/brazil-candidate-bolsonaro-minimizes-slavery-praises-trump; Lempp, "Jair Bolsonaro and Affirmative Action: Political Rupture or Escalation?"

252 Dischino, "Affirmative Action in Brazil: Reverse Discrimination and the Creation of a Constitutionally Protected Color-Line," 170; Constituicao Federal [C.F.] [Constitution] art. 113, § 1 (Braz.).

253 Dischino, "Affirmative Action in Brazil: Reverse Discrimination and the Creation of a Constitutionally Protected Color-Line," 170; Constituicao Federal [C.F.] [Constitution] art. 122, § 1 (1937); Constituicao Federal [C.F.] [Constitution] art. 141, § 1 (1946).

254 Dischino, "Affirmative Action in Brazil: Reverse Discrimination and the Creation of a Constitutionally Protected Color-Line," 170; Constituicao Federal [C.F.] [Constitution] art. 150, § 1 (1967).

255 Tanya Monique Washington, "All Things Being Equal: The Promise of Affirmative Efforts to Eradicate Color-Coded Inequality in the United States and Brazil," *National Black Law Journal* 21, no. 1 (2009): 35; Oppenheimer et al. *Comparative Equality & Anti-Discrimination Law*, 256.

256 Dischino, "Affirmative Action in Brazil: Reverse Discrimination and the Creation of a Constitutionally Protected Color-Line," at 171; Constituicao Federal [C.F.] [Constitution] art. 5, (1988).

257 Constituicao Federal [C.F.] [Constitution] art. 3 (1988).

258 Tanya K. Hernández, "Affirmative Action in the Americas," *Americas Quarterly*. 7, no. 3 (2013): 30. Accessed Nov. 11, 2018. https://www.americasquarterly.org/affirmative-action-in-the-americas.

campaigns to raise awareness of racial discrimination and the socioeconomic exclusion of Afro-Brazilians.[259]

In the mid-1990s, bolstered by international networks, the Afro-Brazilian movement placed intense pressure on the federal government and its diplomats, leading the country to adopt progressive positions.[260] Examples of these positions included an explicit commitment to compensatory policies for the African descendant population and what would later become the National Affirmative Action Program.[261]

In 1999, in Porto Alegre (Brazil's sixth-largest city), the municipal government passed a regulation mandating that the work force of all publicly funded contracts with the city be at least 5 percent *negro* (Black).[262] In the same year, the state government of Bahia (with a 75 percent non-white population) adopted legislation requiring one-third of all models and actors in state publicity to be Black.[263]

In 2001, the federal government began instituting affirmative action policies.[264] The Minister of Agrarian Development, Raul Jungmann, issued an executive order reserving 20 percent of administrative positions in the ministry and 20 percent of staff positions in firms contracting with the agency for Black Brazilians.[265] The order also reserved another 20 percent of the firms' staff positions for women."[266] During the same year, the Supreme Court's affirmative action program set a 20 percent Black quota for public-sector contractors.[267] And the Ministry of Justice's affirmative action program reserved 20 percent of supervisory and upper-level advisory positions for Black and Pardo (Brown) Brazilians.[268]

In 2002, President Fernando Henrique Cardoso issued an executive decree establishing the National Affirmative Action Program to foster implementation of percentage-based goals for Afro-descendants in federal agencies and

259 Ibid.

260 Dischino, "Affirmative Action in Brazil: Reverse Discrimination and the Creation of a Constitutionally Protected Color-Line," 162–163; Martins, Medeiros and Nascimento, "Paving Paradise: the Road from "Racial Democracy" to Affirmative Action in Brazil," 802.

261 Dischino, "Affirmative Action in Brazil: Reverse Discrimination and the Creation of a Constitutionally Protected Color-Line," 163; Martins, Medeiros and Nascimento, "Paving Paradise: the Road from "Racial Democracy" to Affirmative Action in Brazil," 802–803.

262 Hernández, "Affirmative Action in the Americas," 30.

263 Ibid.

264 Ibid.

265 Ibid.

266 Ibid.

267 Ibid.

268 Ibid.

their contracting firms.[269] After the election of President Luiz Inacio Lula da Silva ('Lula') in 2002, the federal government created the Federal Secretariat for Policies Promoting Racial Equality (SEPPIR).[270] The Lula administration, specifically its Ministry of Education, published the National Policy of Racial Equality, which emphasized the need for ongoing development of a comprehensive affirmative action program.[271]

In 2007, the Supreme Federal Court upheld affirmative action in a case involving a physically disabled person seeking public employment under a state public-service quota system.[272] Although speaking in the context of disability affirmative action, the Court articulated general and broad holdings: "the reparation or compensation of the factors creating inequality has been 'inscribed' in Brazil's 'fraternal society' since the publication of the Preamble to the 1988 Constitution" and "the question of equality, although difficult to comprehend, was, without a doubt observed under state law, valorizing the call for affirmative action, a mechanism that defends material and substantive equality."[273]

In 2008, in a case titled *S. T.J., RMS 26.089 – PR 2008/0003014-1*, the Supreme Court of Justice issued the most important case on affirmative action in Brazilian jurisprudence, finding not only that affirmative action was constitutionally permissible, but also that it was constitutionally mandatory. The Court defined affirmative action as a "compulsory, voluntary and facilitating set of public and private policies designed to combat racial discrimination, and to correct the practices of discrimination practiced throughout history."[274] According to the judges, such a system is necessary until the socioeconomic factors benefitting dominant social groups can be eliminated.[275]

269 Ibid.

270 Dischino, "Affirmative Action in Brazil: Reverse Discrimination and the Creation of a Constitutionally Protected Color-Line," 166; Martins, Medeiros and Nascimento, "Paving Paradise: the Road from "Racial Democracy" to Affirmative Action in Brazil," 806.

271 Dischino, "Affirmative Action in Brazil: Reverse Discrimination and the Creation of a Constitutionally Protected Color-Line," 166; Martins, Medeiros and Nascimento, "Paving Paradise: the Road from "Racial Democracy" to Affirmative Action in Brazil," 806.

272 Dischino, "Affirmative Action in Brazil: Reverse Discrimination and the Creation of a Constitutionally Protected Color-Line," 176; S.T.F., RMS 26.071-1/DF, Relator: Min. Carlos Britto, 13.11.2007, R.S.T.F., 314 (Brazil).

273 Dischino, "Affirmative Action in Brazil: Reverse Discrimination and the Creation of a Constitutionally Protected Color-Line," 176; S.T.F., RMS 26.071-1/DF, Relator: Min. Carlos Britto, 13.11.2007, R.S.T.F., 314 (Brazil).

274 Dischino, "Affirmative Action in Brazil: Reverse Discrimination and the Creation of a Constitutionally Protected Color-Line," 178; S.T.J., RMS 26.089 – PR 2008/0003014-1 (translation by author).

275 Dischino, "Affirmative Action in Brazil: Reverse Discrimination and the Creation of a Constitutionally Protected Color-Line," 179; S.T.J., RMS 26.089 – PR 2008/0003014-1 (translation by author).

The Court upheld a state quota for persons of African descent seeking public service positions at the State University of West Paraná's teaching hospital.[276] The plaintiffs (candidates for the positions) brought suit against the Chancellor, arguing that the state law reserving positions for Afro-descendants violated the constitutional principle of equality between candidates ("without distinction as to color, sex, or race").[277] The Court defended the quota as consistent with the National Affirmative Action Program encompassing federal employment, public service, and university admissions.[278] The Court noted that "two notions of equality are present in the text of the Brazilian Constitution: formal equality and material equality."[279] First, formal equality consists of "the necessity to prohibit the State from engaging in discriminatory treatment, and prohibits all administrative, legislative, and judicial acts that deprive one of the right to enjoy fundamental public liberties on the basis of arbitrary criteria."[280] On the other hand, material equality "consists not only of the abolition of arbitrary discrimination, but also the imposition on the State of an affirmative obligation to promote equal opportunity and access to public resources for underrepresented or less favored groups, such as [B]lacks."[281] In terms of the latter (material equality), the goal is to compensate for and eliminate inequalities that have developed over time and are embedded in "cultural sedimentation."[282] The Court found that the 1988 Constitution

276 Dischino, "Affirmative Action in Brazil: Reverse Discrimination and the Creation of a Constitutionally Protected Color-Line," 174; Oppenheimer et al., *Comparative Equality & Anti-Discrimination Law*, 257.

277 Dischino, "Affirmative Action in Brazil: Reverse Discrimination and the Creation of a Constitutionally Protected Color-Line," 174; S.T.J., RMS 26.089 PR 2008/0003014-1, Relator: Min. Felix Fischer, 12.05.2008; Oppenheimer et al., *Comparative Equality & Anti-Discrimination Law*, 257.

278 Dischino, "Affirmative Action in Brazil: Reverse Discrimination and the Creation of a Constitutionally Protected Color-Line," 174; S.T.J., RMS 26.089 PR 2008/0003014-1, Relator: Min. Felix Fischer, 12.05.2008; Oppenheimer et al., *Comparative Equality & Anti-Discrimination Law*, 257.

279 Dischino, "Affirmative Action in Brazil: Reverse Discrimination and the Creation of a Constitutionally Protected Color-Line," at 175; S.T.J., RMS 26.089 PR 2008/0003014-1, Relator: Min. Felix Fischer, 12.05.2008.

280 Dischino, "Affirmative Action in Brazil: Reverse Discrimination and the Creation of a Constitutionally Protected Color-Line," at 175; S.T.J., RMS 26.089 PR 2008/0003014-1, Relator: Min. Felix Fischer, 12.05.2008.

281 Dischino, "Affirmative Action in Brazil: Reverse Discrimination and the Creation of a Constitutionally Protected Color-Line," 175; S.T.J., RMS 26.089 PR 2008/0003014-1, Relator: Min. Felix Fischer, 12.05.2008.

282 Dischino, "Affirmative Action in Brazil: Reverse Discrimination and the Creation of a Constitutionally Protected Color-Line," 175; S.T.J., RMS 26.089 PR 2008/0003014-1, Relator: Min. Felix Fischer, 12.05.2008.

not only created the possibility of, but also imposed a constitutional duty for, State-mandated affirmative action.[283] The Court concluded that the affirmative action policies were necessary because Brazil had committed itself to promoting policies eliminating "racism, preconceptions, discrimination, and lack of opportunities for Afro-descendants."[284]

In June 2011, Rio de Janeiro's state government issued a decree reserving 20 percent of vacancies in exams for civil service positions in the state government for Black people and persons of Indigenous descent.[285]

1.7 *Positive Measures in Employment in Europe*

The first major pan-European commitment to equality can be seen in Article 14 of the European Convention on Human Rights, which entered into force on September 3rd, 1953 and is slowly growing from a relatively toothless provision into a mandate for substantive equality.[286] The 1957 Treaty of Rome required the original six member-states of what became the European Union (Belgium, Germany, France, Italy, Luxembourg, and the Netherlands) to provide for gender equality regarding pay (Art. 119).[287] In 1976, the Council of the European Communities issued Directive 76/207/EEC permitting "measures to promote equal opportunity for men and women, in particular by removing existing inequalities which affect women's opportunities."[288] In 1984 the Council explicitly recommended that member states engage in "positive action policies" to "promote a better balance between the sexes in employment."[289]

In 2000, the European Union's then-15-member states unanimously adopted two equality directives, the Racial Equality Directive – EC Council Directive

283 Dischino, "Affirmative Action in Brazil: Reverse Discrimination and the Creation of a Constitutionally Protected Color-Line," 175; S.T.J., RMS 26.089 PR 2008/0003014-1, Relator: Min. Felix Fischer, 12.05.2008.

284 Dischino, "Affirmative Action in Brazil: Reverse Discrimination and the Creation of a Constitutionally Protected Color-Line," 175; S.T.J., RMS 26.089 PR 2008/0003014-1, Relator: Min. Felix Fischer, 12.05.2008.

285 Hernández, "Affirmative Action in the Americas," 30.

286 Sandra Fredman, "Emerging from the Shadows: Substantive Equality and Article 14 of the European Convention on Human Rights," *Human Rights Law Review* 16, no. 2 (2016): 301. doi:10.1093/hrlr/ngw001.

287 *See* Sylvia Walby. "The European Union and gender equality: Emergent varieties of gender regime," *Social Politics: International Studies in Gender, State & Society* 11, no. 1 (2004): 17–20.

288 Council Directive 76/207/EEC of 9 February 1976 on the implementation of the principle of equal treatment for men and women as regards access to employment, vocational training and promotion, and working conditions, Feb. 9, 1976, 1976 O.J. (L 39) 40.

289 *See* 84/635/EEC: Council recommendation of 13 December 1984 on the promotion of positive action for women, 1984 OJ (L 331) 34.

2000/43/EC of 29 June 2000,[290] and the Employment Equality Directive – EC Council Directive 2000/78/EC of 27 November 2000.[291]

The Racial Equality Directive provides that "the purpose of this Directive is to lay down a framework for combating discrimination on the grounds of racial or ethnic origin, with a view to putting into effect in the Member States the principle of equal treatment" (Art. 1) and that "with a view to ensuring full equality in practice, the principle of equal treatment shall not prevent any Member State from maintaining or adopting specific measures to prevent or compensate for disadvantages linked to racial or ethnic origin" (Art. 5). In keeping with these requirements, EU legislation mandates Member States prohibit racial discrimination in employment, education, healthcare, and housing.[292] To supplement this, EU institutions have also made commitments to opposing racism in all areas of EU law and policy as part of a policy of mainstreaming antiracist policies.[293]

The Employment Equality Directive provides that the "purpose of this Directive is to lay down a general framework for combating discrimination on the grounds of religion or belief, disability, age or sexual orientation as regards employment and occupation, with a view to putting into effect in the Member States the principle of equal treatment" (Art. 1) and that with "a view to ensuring full equality in practice, the principle of equal treatment shall not prevent any Member State from maintaining or adopting specific measures to prevent or compensate for disadvantages linked to any of the grounds referred to in Article 1" (Art. 7).

Early decisions of the European Court of Justice (subsequently renamed the Court of Justice of the European Union), the European Union's high court, held that affirmative action programs designed to create opportunities for women in the workforce violated European law because the court framed European equality law as requiring formal equality. In *Eckhard Kalanke v. Freie Hansestadt Bremen* (1995),[294] the Court rejected a German civil service preference for women. The Court held that Article 2(1) and (4) of the Directive

---

290 Council Directive 2000/43/EC of 29 June 2000 implementing the principle of equal treatment between persons irrespective of racial or ethnic origin, 2000 OJ (L 180) 22.

291 Council Directive 2000/78/EC of 27 November 2000 establishing a general framework for equal treatment in employment and occupation, 2000 OJ (L 303) 16.

292 *See generally* Mark Bell, *Racism and Equality in the European Union.* (Oxford: Oxford University Press, 2009). Oxford Scholarship Online, 2009. doi:10.1093/acprof:oso/9780199297849.001.0001.

293 *See generally* Ibid.

294 C-450/93, *Kalanke v. Bremen*, 1995 ECR I-3051.

precludes national rules that automatically give priority to women in sectors where they are under-represented. The *Kalanke* ruling created upheaval and considerable uncertainty among experts and States about the legitimacy of quotas and other preferential measures to advance the professional position of women.[295] But the European Commission pushed back, publishing a Communication in March 1996 to clarify that *Kalanke* only concerned strict quotas, and that other types of positive action measures are permissible in EU law, as the *Kalanke* ruling was based on the rigid nature of the German law, and did not adequately account for different contexts.[296] Accordingly, the Communication asserted that most affirmative action measures could be allowed provided they were not automatic and accounted for the current context.[297] In particular, the Communication established that quotas linked to the qualifications required for the job may be acceptable, as long as they account for contextual circumstances that could justify an exception to the principle of giving preference to the underrepresented sex.[298]

In the ensuing years, the institutions of the EU have taken an increasingly assertive role in promoting gender equality in the workplace. The European Court of Justice now justifies positive action, beginning with the *Hellmut Marschall v. Land Nordrhein-Westfalen* (1997) case, based on the need to remedy existing sex discrimination. *Hellmuth Marschall*[299] held that in a case where there are fewer women than men at the level of the relevant post in a sector of the public service, and both female and male candidates for the post are equally qualified, the employer may give priority to the promotion of female candidates unless reasons specific to an individual male candidate tilt the balance in his favor. Such tie-breaking by gender is not precluded by Article 2(1) and (4) of the Sex Equality Directive, provided that the candidatures will be the subject of an objective assessment that will take account of all criteria specific to the individual candidates and will override the priority accorded to female candidates where one or more of those criteria tilts the balance in favor of the male candidate.[300] The Court explained:[301]

---

295 Ibid.

296 *See* European Commission Communication The interpretation of the judgment of the Court of Justice on 17 October 1995 in Case C-450/93, *Kalanke v. Freie Hansestadt Bremen*, COM (96) 88 final, 1, 3, 6 and 8–10.

297 Ibid.

298 Ibid. at 9.

299 C-409/95, *Marschall v. Land Nordrhein-Westfalen*, 1997 E.C.R. I-6363 (1997).

300 Ibid.

301 Ibid. at para 29.

> [I]t appears that even where male and female candidates are equally qualified, male candidates tend to be promoted in preference to female candidates particularly because of prejudices and stereotypes concerning the role and capacities of women in working life and the fear, for example, that women will interrupt their careers more frequently, that owing to household and family duties they will be less flexible in their working hours, or that they will be absent from work more frequently because of pregnancy, childbirth and breastfeeding ... For these reasons, the mere fact that a male candidate and a female candidate are equally qualified does not mean that they have the same chances.[302]

Thus, on this basis the court allowed gender to serve as a tie breaker when determining who should receive a promotion.[303]

In *Georg Badeck and Others* (2000), the court moved beyond its *Marshall* ruling. The decision authorized the permissibility of a national rule adopted on the basis of articles 2.1 and 2.4 of the Original Gender Equal Treatment Directive that allocated at least half of the training places to women in trained occupations where women are underrepresented, and for which the States lack monopoly of training to eliminate such underrepresentation.[304]

The Council of Europe also has jurisdiction over some inequality issues. Its European Commission against Racism and Intolerance (ECRI) is composed of independent experts who monitor and examine manifestations of racism and intolerance in each of the Council of Europe member states.[305] Its General Policy Recommendation No. 7 of 2002, on national legislation to combat racism and racial discrimination, states:

> The law should provide that the prohibition of racial discrimination does not prevent the maintenance or adoption of temporary special measures designed either to prevent or compensate for disadvantages suffered by persons designated by the grounds (race, color, language religion, nationality or national or ethnic origin), or to facilitate their full participation in all fields of life. These measures should not be continued once the intended objectives have been achieved.

302 Ibid.

303 Ibid.

304 C-158/97, Georg Badeck and others, 2000 ECR I-1875 (2000) at par. 53–55.

305 European Commission against Racism and Intolerance (ECRI), *General Policy Recommendation No. 7: National Legislation to Combat Racism and Racial Discrimination*. Strasbourg: ECRI, 2017, para. 5.

The European Committee on Social Rights (ECSR) monitors the implementation of the anti-discrimination provision contained in article E of the Revised European Social Charter of 1996.[306] The ECSR includes a positive obligation for States to take positive action to promote substantive equality for disadvantaged groups, such as the Roma, in addition to a negative obligation not to discriminate.[307]

Across Europe, the unemployment rates of Roma communities, and especially of Roma women, are considerably higher than those of other groups, and studies indicate that Roma are highly discriminated against in the labor market.[308] The Advisory Committee on the Framework Convention for the Protection of National Minorities (ACFC) identifies positive action as one key to reaching full and effective equality for Roma in employment and "supports efforts to seek financing for such measures."[309] The European Commission suggests that Public Employment Services can reach out to the Roma by providing personalized services and mediation to promote the employment of qualified Roma civil servants in the public sector.[310] The Parliamentary Assembly of the Council of Europe (CoE) cites special internship programs for Roma in the civil service as an appropriate means to increase the representation of members of Roma communities in State and local administrations.[311] The European Commission provides positive measures for Roma workers by reserving a specific number of traineeships exclusively for Roma graduates next to its general

306 *See generally* Colm O'Cinneide, "The European Social Charter and the UK: Why it Matters," *King's Law Journal* 29, no. 2, (2018): 275–296. https://doi.org/10.1080/09615768.2018.1502064.

307 Jozefien Van Caeneghem, "The Use of Ethnic Data Collection and Positive Action to Combat Discrimination and Promote Equality and Social Inclusion of the Roma Minority in Europe," (PhD diss., Vrije Universiteit Brussel, 2017), 349.

308 World Bank. 2010. *Roma inclusion: An economic opportunity for Bulgaria, Czech Republic, Romania and Serbia (English)*. Washington D.C.: World Bank. http://documents.worldbank.org/curated/en/196921468261335364/Roma-inclusion-An-economic-opportunity-for-Bulgaria-Czech-Republic-Romania-and-Serbia.

309 Council of Europe, *Advisory Committee on the Framework Convention for the Protection of National Minorities, First Opinion on Serbia and Montenegro*, Strasbourg: Council of Europe, 2003, ACFC/INF/OP/I (2004)002, par. 38.

310 Van Caeneghem, "The Use of Ethnic Data Collection and Positive Action to Combat Discrimination and Promote Equality and Social Inclusion of the Roma Minority in Europe," 397.

311 Council of Europe, "The Situation of Roma in Europe and Relevant Activities of the Council of Europe," Parliamentary Assembly, June 22, 2010, art. 18.4. Accessed February 15, 2019. http://assembly.coe.int/nw/xml/XRef/Xref-XML2HTML-en.asp?fileid=17875&lang=en.

traineeship, to allow Roma to gain familiarity with working at the EU and acquire the relevant competences for future recruitment.[312]

In 2004, a group of French companies, now numbering over 3,800, launched the "Diversity Charter" initiative.[313] The Charter is intended to demonstrate a commitment to cultural, ethnic, and social diversity within French organizations. The signatories agree, in charter section 3, to "endeavor to reflect the diversity of the French society particularly in its cultural and ethnic dimension at every level of our workforce."[314]

Subsequently, Diversity Charters were adopted in several forms in 16 European states, with the support of many private and public employers. The Charters provide a commitment by its signatories to a number of positive measures to increase workforce diversity.[315] Every Diversity Charter text is adapted to a country's national culture as well as to its specific priorities and concerns.[316] That said, all of the European Diversity Charters have certain common objectives, such as raising awareness of the importance of diversity and its socio-economic impact; and bringing together all stakeholders, including companies, local governments, organizations combating discrimination, associations, and the academy.[317]

In the United Kingdom, Section 149 of the Equality Act of 2010, the Public Sector Equality Duty, came into force on April 5, 2011.[318] In the exercise of their functions, public authorities in England, Scotland and Wales must pay "due regard to the need to eliminate unlawful discrimination, harassment and

312 European Agency for Fundamental Rights, "Roma Internship," *European Agency for Fundamental Rights*, accessed November 11, 2018. http://fra.europa.eu/en/vacancy/2017/roma-internship-programme-2017–2018.

313 "La Charte De La Diversité," Charte De La Diversité | Charte De La Diversité. 2018. Accessed February 10, 2019. https://www.charte-diversite.com/charte-de-la-diversite/.

314 Ibid.

315 Ibid.

316 *See* Ibid; *See also* "Diversity Charters in Europe," Diversity Journal, August 28, 2012, accessed February 10, 2019. http://www.diversityjournal.com/9762-diversity-charters-in-europe/.

317 "EU Platform of Diversity Charters," The European Commission, August 1, 2018, accessed February 10, 2019. https://ec.europa.eu/info/policies/justice-and-fundamental-rights/combatting-discrimination/tackling-discrimination/diversity-management/eu-platform-diversity-charters_en.

318 James Hand, Bernard Davis, and Pat Feast, "Unification, simplification, amplification? An analysis of aspects of the British Equality Act 2010," *Commonwealth Law Bulletin* 38, no. 3 (2012): 510; UK Parliament, *Equality Act of 2010*, London: Legislation.gov.uk. Accessed February 21, 2019. https://www.legislation.gov.uk/ukpga/2010/15. (Section 217 establishes that for the most part this act does not apply to Northern Ireland.)

victimisation and other conduct prohibited by the Act,"[319] and "to advance equality of opportunity between people who share a protected characteristic and those who do not."[320] There is an open question regarding whether or not this requires positive measures.[321] The equality duty covers nine protected characteristics: age, disability, gender reassignment, pregnancy and maternity, race, religion or belief, sex, and sexual orientation.[322]

Northern Ireland's Fair Employment Act of 1989 imposes on all regulated employers, both public and private, a duty to carry out regular reviews of the composition of their workforce to determine whether or not there is fair employment, and to undertake remedial action where required.[323] These reviews enable the Equality Commission to identify employers with homogenous workforces and work with them to develop a program to rectify the problem.[324] The majority of the workplace programs that have been established have been meant to remedy Catholic underrepresentation, though there have also been a number designed to remedy Protestant underrepresentation in specific regulated employers.[325]

Before France amended the 1987 Disability Employment Act in 2005, the inclusion of persons with disabilities in mainstream employment was mostly pursued through affirmative action, in the form of a quota scheme.[326] This system was initially created for war-disabled veterans after the First World War, (*mutilés de guerre ou autres infirmes*) and then extended to other people with disabilities. The Act of July 10, 1987 "in favor of employment of disabled people" (*Loi n°-87-517 du 10 juillet 1987 en faveur de l'emploi des travailleurs handicapés*) introduced the "employment obligation."[327] The obligation requires private companies of twenty or more employees (*travailleurs salariés*)

319 Hand, Davis, and Feast, "Unification, simplification, amplification? An analysis of aspects of the British Equality Act 2010," 510.

320 Ibid. at 512.

321 Ibid. at 513.

322 Ibid.

323 Christopher McCrudden, Raya Muttarak, Heather Hamill, and Anthony Heath, "Affirmative action without quotas in Northern Ireland," *The Equal Rights Review* 4, (2009): 9. http://www.equalrightstrust.org/ertdocumentbank/err_issue04%20christopher.pdf.

324 Ibid. at 8.

325 Ibid. at 9.

326 Thomas Barnay, Emmanuel Duguet, Christine Le Clainche, and Yann Videau, "An evaluation of the 1987 French Disabled Workers Act: Better paying than hiring," *hal-01260162* (2016): 2. https://hal.archives-ouvertes.fr/hal-01260162/document.

327 Loi n° 87-517 du 10 juillet 1987 en faveur de l'emploi des travailleurs handicapés [Law No. 87-517 of 10 July 1987 on the employment of disabled workers] Journal Officiel De La Republique Francaise [J.O.] [Official Gazette of France], July 12, 1987, p. 7822.

to directly employ workers with disabilities as at least six percent of their workforce.[328] The Act provides employers (duty-bearers) with a few alternatives to the six-percent quota, such as permitting a company to contract out some of its activities to non-mainstream employment structures designed for the employment of persons with disabilities.[329] Non-compliant duty-bearers must pay a "financial contribution" to an association managing a fund to promote the inclusion of workers with disabilities.[330] The amount of the contribution takes the minimum wage as a basis of calculation and varies according to the company's size and the number of workers with disabilities that it should be employing.[331] The following fines are assessed to corporations that do not fulfill the six-percent quota: 3904 EUR (for companies of 20 to 199 workers); 4880 EUR (200 to 749 workers); 5856 EUR (750+ workers).[332] Because the fine, at under ten euros per employee, is low, many employers pay it rather than hire employees with disabilities.[333]

1.8 *Positive Measures in Employment in Colombia*

Despite widespread discrimination, until recently Afro-Colombian social movements were not integrated into national politics.[334] Within the framework of liberal ideologies of citizenship, the *negro* category played no role in state practices.[335] Academics paid no attention to "Black" as a category: anthropology focused on indigenous peoples; sociology centered on peasants and social classes.[336] Black Colombians have been and still are disproportionately impoverished and densely concentrated in certain regions, resulting in de facto regional segregation.[337] Afro-Colombians are plagued by, among other things, "high rates of informal labor and unemployment, high dropout rates, illiteracy, overcrowding, poor access to potable water, poor sanitation, child labor, and

328 Ibid.
329 Ibid.
330 Ibid.
331 Ibid.
332 Ibid.
333 Barnay et al., "An evaluation of the 1987 French Disabled Workers Act: Better paying than hiring," 13–15.
334 Tianna S. Paschel, "The Right to Difference: Explaining Colombia's Shift from Color Blindness to the Law of Black Communities," *American Journal of Sociology* 116, no. 3 (2010): 730.
335 Peter Wade, "Defining Blackness in Colombia," *Journal de la Société des Américanistes* 95, no. 1 (2009): 167.
336 Ibid.
337 Paschel, "The Right to Difference: Explaining Colombia's Shift from Color Blindness to the Law of Black Communities," 737.

poor access to government services."[338] According to the 2005 census, 10.6% of the population is Afro-Colombian, but Benjy Hansen-Bundy estimates that the actual number could be as high as 25% because of how mixed-race individuals self-identify.[339] In 2010, Gay McDougall (the UN Independent Expert on minority issues) noted that although the constitutional and legislative measures deserve praise, the implementation of Colombia's laws on Afro-Colombian communities remains "woefully inadequate, limited and sporadic."[340]

The movement for affirmative action in Colombia began in the 1970s, when, inspired by U.S. Black activism and the South African anti-apartheid movement, Black student activist groups began to form."[341] Then, in the late 1980s, Black Colombian organizations began demanding recognition and rights as an ethnic group.[342] In 1991, Colombia adopted a new constitution officially recognizing the country as "pluri-ethnic" and "multicultural" and establishing protections for ethnic and cultural diversity.[343] The 1991 Colombian Constitution in Article 13 ("Fundamental Rights") states:

> All individuals are born free and equal before the law, will receive equal protection and treatment from the authorities, and will enjoy the same rights, freedoms, and opportunities without any discrimination on account of gender, race, national or family origin, language, religion, political opinion, or philosophy.[344]
>
> The State will promote the conditions so that equality may be real and effective and will adopt measures in favor of groups that are discriminated against or marginalized.[345]
>
> The State will especially protect those individuals who on account of their economic, physical, or mental condition are in obviously vulnerable circumstances and will sanction the abuses or ill-treatment perpetrated against them.[346]

---

338 Benjy Hansen-Bundy, "Afro-Colombians battle racism and socio-economic exclusion," *Colombia Reports*. March 22, 2013, accessed October 29, 2017. https://colombiareports.com/afro-colombians-battle-racism-and-socio-economic-exclusion/.

339 Ibid.

340 Ibid.

341 Wade, "Defining Blackness in Colombia," 168.

342 Paschel, "The Right to Difference: Explaining Colombia's Shift from Color Blindness to the Law of Black Communities," 737–738.

343 Ibid. at 730.

344 Constitucion Politica De Colombia [C.P.], art. 13. https://www.constituteproject.org/constitution/Colombia_2005.pdf.

345 Ibid.

346 Ibid.

Thus, the state is not only allowed to implement affirmative action programs but is in fact required to implement affirmative action programs on behalf of the disadvantaged.

In 1993, mandated by the 1991 Constitution, Law 70 (the Law of Black Communities) was adopted.[347] Tianna Paschel argues it is the most comprehensive legislation for Black populations in all of Latin America.[348] The two main objectives of Law 70 were to "recognize and guarantee collective land rights to black Colombian communities living in a specific rural region on the Pacific Coast of Colombia and establish mechanisms for the protection of the socioeconomic and cultural rights of Black Colombians and of their equality."[349] Among the changes introduced were the mandatory incorporation of Afro-Colombian history in the educational curriculum and the right to be consulted on development projects that affect them.[350] In addition, "Afro-Colombian communities on the Pacific coast were granted collective titles to land occupied by their ancestors when slavery was abolished in 1851."[351]

In 2000, in a case titled Decision *C-371* of 2000, the Supreme Court upheld a gender quota law and defined affirmative action as "policies or measures aimed at favoring specific people or groups, whether to eliminate or reduce social, cultural, or economic inequalities affecting them or to achieve greater inclusion for member of underprivileged groups, usually those subject to discrimination."[352] The Court posed the question of whether the legislator may grant preferential treatment in the distribution of goods, rights, or obligations based on the recipient's sex.[353] The Court responded that, without a doubt, the answer must be drawn from Article 13 of the Constitution.[354]

Drawing on the case law of the U.S. Supreme Court, the Court stated that classifications involving suspect classes will be particularly heavily scrutinized.[355] The Court clarified that whenever "such characteristics or

347 Paschel, "The Right to Difference: Explaining Colombia's Shift from Color Blindness to the Law of Black Communities," 730.

348 Ibid.

349 Ibid. at 738.

350 Ibid. at 730; "Affirmative Action in Colombia: Debating Quotas," *The Economist*. July 30, 2009, accessed October 29, 2017. http://www.economist.com/node/14140625.

351 "Affirmative Action in Colombia: Debating Quotas."

352 Manuel José Cepeda Espinosa and David Lanau, *Colombian Constitutional Law: Leading Cases* (Oxford: Oxford University Press, 2017), 102.

353 Ibid.

354 Ibid.

355 Ibid. at 84.

factors are invoked in order to establish differences regarding treatment, an infringement on the right to equality is assumed."[356]

However, departing from the U.S. doctrine, the Court held that "affirmative action measures aiding historically-disadvantaged groups should be treated as less suspect than measures discriminating against those groups."[357] "[C]lause 2 of Article 13 establishes that 'the state shall promote the conditions so that equality may be real and effective and shall adopt measures in favor of groups which are discriminated against or marginalized.'"[358] Therefore, affirmative action is clearly authorized by the Constitution, and authorities may invoke race, sex, or any other suspicious category not for the sake of exclusion or perpetuation of inequalities, but rather to reduce the harmful effects of social behaviors that have subjugated these groups in unfavorable conditions.[359] The fact remains that the State cannot effectively attempt to improve the situation of a marginalized group without mentioning the factor that provoked that segregation.[360] Therefore, "if the law seeks to improve the status of women ..., or indigenous groups ..., it must resort to ethnic or sex based classifications."[361]

The court clarified that the Constitutional validity of these measures depends on the actual presence of discrimination,[362] and that each situation must be examined on a case-by-case basis to see if the discriminatory treatment established is "reasonable and fair."[363] The Court further held that affirmative action should be temporary because once "real and effective equality" have been achieved, it is no longer necessary.[364]

In 2012, the Colombia Ministry of the Interior proposed a law based on the recommendations of the Commission for the advancement of Afro-Colombian people, created by the government in October 2007.[365] The law was meant to address the low rate of Afro-Colombian representation in government by having the Ministry of the Interior mandate government agencies and political

---

356 Ibid. at 102.
357 Ibid. at 84–85.
358 Ibid. at 103.
359 Ibid.
360 Ibid.
361 Ibid.
362 Ibid.
363 Ibid.
364 Ibid.
365 Colombian Ministry of the Interior, *PROYECTO DE LEY ESTATUTARIA No ____ de 2012*. Bogota: Ministry of the Interior, 2012. Accessed November 12, 2018. https://www.mininterior.gov.co/sites/default/files/noticias/por_el_cual_se_establece_la_ley_de_participacion_y_representacion_para_las_comunidades_negras_afrocolombianas_raizales_y_palenqueras.pdf.

parties to include affirmative action programs in their hiring and create a "Certificate of Ethnic Responsibility" that would be awarded to all private and public companies who employed at least 10% minorities.[366] Finally, the law would have mandated that 10% of scholarships go to racial minorities, such that minorities would represent 10% of the student body for institutions of higher education by 2024.[367] However, the proposal was not enacted.[368]

In the area of gender-based affirmative action, Colombia has made great strides over the past two decades, starting in 2000 with the Ley de Cuotas (Quota Law), which established a 30% employment quota for women in the public sector, which the Colombian Supreme Court upheld "as an attempt to transform the political sphere by overcoming entrenched historical barriers to the participation of women in public life" through measures to increase women's participation in public sector decision-making.[369] Beyond that, the Ley de Cuotas was important on two levels.[370] The first was that in being ruled constitutional by the Colombian Supreme Court, the court also held that the quota should extend to representation in electoral politics (though the actual implementation of that would come in later legislation).[371] The second was that it served as a powerful symbol in Colombia for the legitimacy of women's equality.[372] This greater focus has in turn led to numerous effects ranging from greater efforts to combat sexual violence, a greater focus on women's issues in the political discourse, and eventually the enactment of further affirmative action laws such as the "First Job Act," which reduces the tax burden for employers hiring women over 40 who have not had employment contracts in the past 12 months and single mothers with low socioeconomic levels, in a bid to further improve gender equality.[373]

366 Ibid.

367 Ibid.

368 Ibid.

369 Espinosa and Lanau, *Colombian Constitutional Law: Leading Cases*, 101–102.

370 Pilar Domingo, Alina Rocha Menocal, Verónica Hinestroza, "PROGRESS DESPITE ADVERSITY: Women's empowerment and conflict in Colombia," (Developmentprogress .org, 2015), 25–26. https://www.odi.org/sites/odi.org.uk/files/odi-assets/publications -opinion-files/9743.pdf.

371 Ibid. (More on this in the section on parity democracy.)

372 Ibid.

373 Ibid.; Miguel Camilo Ruiz Blanco, "Deputy Permanent Representative of Colombia to the United Nations Colombia's Statement to the Fifty-Seventh Session of the UN Commission on the Status of Women," (Statement, Fifty-Seventh Session of the UN Commission on the Status of Women, NY, March 15, 2013).

1.9 *Conclusion: Positive Measures in Employment*

In conclusion, around the globe positive measures in employment by their many names (affirmative action, positive action, compensatory action, reservations, positive measures, special measures, set-asides) are ubiquitous. Sometimes they take the form of hard quotas (India, Brazil, South Africa, Colombia, France). Other times they take the form of soft quotas (Canada, the U.S., the E.U.). At times they are mandatory (several international conventions, Brazil, India) – at other times merely permissible (the E.U., the U.S.). With the exception of hard quotas, the argument that they violate the anti-discrimination principle is nearly uniformly rejected. Yet there is a clear tension, as many systems require that positive measures be framed as temporary, to avoid a perpetual system of hiring by quota. Such measures are frequently seen as an affirmative effort to – on the one hand, avoid discrimination, and – on the other hand, provide a remedy for discrimination. Quotas are nearly uniformly controversial and divide those who support substantive equality from those who insist on formal equality. But many positive measure programs are generally non-controversial, including outreach programs; mentoring programs; training programs; diversity programs, equity and inclusion programs; di-biasing programs, goals and timetables; and assessment programs. And finally, regardless of their legal status, affirmative measure programs can be political lightning rods, as we are seeing at the moment in India, Brazil, and the United States.

Part 2: Positive Measures in Higher Education

In the twentieth century and today, around the globe, education is widely seen as the pathway from poverty to the middle class and higher education the path to the professional or upper class. Thus, as discriminatory policies that kept schools closed to minorities were lifted, and as universities began to adopt programs to admit students from previously excluded minority groups, majority groups pushed back. Even more than in employment, special measures in admission to higher education have been controversial. But as this section describes and demonstrates, these policies continue to grow, transforming educational institutions and societies in the process.

2.1 *Positive Measures in Higher Education in the United States*

Prior to the American Civil War, nearly all colleges and universities in the United States excluded Black students, although a few, including Amherst and Bowdoin, admitted a small number.[374] The earliest recorded institution to have an open admission policy was Oberlin College, which began admitting Black students in 1835. The first degree-granting higher education institutions specifically for African Americans were also founded pre-Civil War. The Institute for Colored Youth, in Cheyney, Pennsylvania, was founded in 1837, followed by Lincoln University in 1854 and Wilberforce University in 1857.[375] Before the Civil War, there was but a single interracial educational institution in the South – Kentucky's Berea College, which has been an interracial and coeducational institution since its founding in 1855.[376]

After the Civil War small numbers of Black students were admitted into colleges and medical schools throughout the country,[377] although admission in the South ended with end of Reconstruction in 1877.[378] Even in the North, the period after Reconstruction and before World War II was typified by segregation in all realms of social life, including education, with most Black students who attended college (itself a small number) attending Black colleges.[379] In the "Ivy League," Harvard was exceptional in admitting small yet significant numbers of Black students (as well as Catholics, Jews and other minorities) beginning in the 1860s, in pursuit of a policy of creating diversity in the student body.[380]

374 Robert Samuel Fletcher, *A History of Oberlin College from its Foundation Through the Civil War* (Oberlin, OH: Oberlin University Press, 1943): 178.

375 U.S. Department of Education. *Historically Black Colleges and Universities and Higher Education Desegregation*. Washington D.C.: U.S. Dep't of Education Office for Civil Rights, 1991. Accessed Feb. 23, 2019. https://www2.ed.gov/about/offices/list/ocr/docs/hq9511.html.

376 "Berea College Early History," *Berea College*. Accessed January 12, 2018. https://www.berea.edu/about/history/. (A Kentucky state law prohibiting interracial education prevented Berea from enrolling Black students from 1904 to 1950. When the law was upheld by the U.S. Supreme Court, the college set aside funds to establish the Lincoln Institute for Black students.)

377 "Black History Month: A Medical Perspective: Education," *LibGuides*. Accessed December 21, 2017. http://guides.mclibrary.duke.edu/blackhistorymonth/education; *see also* "Key Events in Black Higher Education: JBHE Chronology of Major Landmarks in the Progress of African Americans in Higher Education," *Journal of Blacks in Higher Education*. Accessed January 12, 2018. https://www.jbhe.com/chronology/.

378 Faustine C. Jones, "Black Americans and the City: A Historical Survey," *Journal of Negro Education* 42, no. 3 (Summer 1973): 265.

379 Ibid.; Frederick Chambers, "Histories of Black Colleges and Universities," *Journal of Negro History* 57, no. 3 (July 1972): 270–275.

380 *See* David B. Oppenheimer, "Archibald Cox and the Diversity Justification for Affirmative Action," *Virginia Journal of Social Policy and the Law* 25, no. 2, (2018): 188–190.

Historically Black colleges remain a pillar of educational and socioeconomic mobility for Black Americans in the United States today; they educate just one percent of the total student population, but about ten percent of all Black college students.[381]

After World War II, restrictions on the admission of Black students began to fall away, except in the South where there was still legally imposed segregation, and admission of African American students, when it occurred, was generally by court order.[382]

In *Sweatt v. Painter* (1950), the Supreme Court held that the Equal Protection Clause of the Fourteenth Amendment required that a Black student be admitted to the University of Texas Law School because a separate institution (created for Black students in response to desegregation litigation) could not provide a legal education that was substantially equal. Key in determining that a segregated law school experience was insufficient was an acknowledgement that a core part of a legal education is the exchange of ideas with peers who would inevitably be one's colleagues in the legal field. The Court noted that "few students and no one who has practiced law would choose to study in an academic vacuum, removed from the interplay of ideas and the exchange of views with which the law is concerned."[383]

A decade after *Sweatt v. Painter*, most colleges and universities in the South remained all-white. In the 1960s, white students rioted, and state governors stridently opposed integration at the University of Mississippi and the University of Alabama.[384] In 1962, 160 U.S. Marshalls were injured, and a French journalist and a bystander were killed by a white mob egged on by Mississippi governor Ross Barnett as the Marshalls tried to protect James Meredith while he attempted to enroll as the first Black student at the University of Mississippi.[385] The following year, Alabama Governor George Wallace personally blocked the doorway of the University of Alabama to prevent Vivian Malone and James Hood from becoming the University's first Black students.[386]

---

381 "Table 306.20. Total Fall enrollment in degree-granting postsecondary institutions, by level, and control of institution and race/ethnicity of students: Selected years, 1976 through 2015," *National Center for Education Statistics*. Accessed Feb. 13, 2018. https://nces.ed.gov/programs/digest/d16/tables/dt16_306.20.asp?current=yes.

382 *Sweatt v. Painter*, 339 U.S. 629, 636 (1950).

383 Ibid. at 634.

384 Taylor Branch, *Parting the Waters: America in the King of Years 1954–63* (New York: Touchstone, 1989): 668–669, 821–822.

385 Ibid.

386 Ibid.

Harvard started affirmatively recruiting Black students in 1948 and dramatically increased its efforts in the late 1950s and early 1960s with the growth of the Civil Rights Movement.[387] In the early 1960s, outside the South, other schools followed, with both private and public schools adopting affirmative action programs to increase the enrollment of Black and other minority students. As their numbers grew, Black students and allied activists led protests on college campuses for student representation proportionate to the Black population, and for increased resources for Black Studies and affinity groups on campuses. Their protests were instrumental in bringing attention and urgency to affirmative action.[388] But there was a price to pay in the form of political backlash (or "whitelash") against them.[389] Nonetheless, through the 1970s colleges and universities continued to develop affirmative action programs and enroll increasing numbers of minorities and women.[390]

In 1974 the first challenge to affirmative action reached the United States Supreme Court in *Defunis v. Odegaard*, but it was dismissed as moot. Marco DeFunis, an unsuccessful applicant to the University of Washington's law school, challenged the law school's efforts to increase minority enrollment.[391] Most of the arguments in support of the University's affirmative action program focused on theories of substantive equality, the need for remedial action, and the need for more Black lawyers. But in a brief on behalf of Harvard College, Archibald Cox, the former U.S. Solicitor General and Watergate Special Prosecutor, argued that the best justification for affirmative action was

387 Dennis Deslippe, *Protesting Affirmative Action: The Struggle over Equality after the Civil Rights Revolution* (Baltimore: Johns Hopkins University Press, 2012): 57; Oppenheimer, "Archibald Cox and the Diversity Justification for Affirmative Action," 19–21.

388 Philip Rubio, *History of Affirmative Action, 1619–2000* (Jackson: University Press of Mississippi, 2001): 128–129; Deslippe, *Protesting Affirmative Action: The Struggle over Equality after the Civil Rights Revolution*, 62–63.

389 *See* Deslippe, *Protesting Affirmative Action: The Struggle over Equality after the Civil Rights Revolution*, 67–78; Dean J. Kotlowski, *Nixon's Civil Rights: Politics, Principle, & Policy* (Cambridge: Harvard University Press, 2009), 116–117; "Whitelash – Neologisms," *The Rice University Neologisms Database*. December 3, 2016, accessed February 24, 2018. http://neologisms.rice.edu/index.php?a=term&d=1&t=20709. (The term "whitelash" refers to "the angry, [at times] violent reaction of some white people as civil rights advocates became more vocal."); Ian Haney López, *Dog Whistle Politics: How Coded Racial Appeals Have Reinvented Racism and Wrecked the Middle Class* (New York: Oxford University Press, 2014): 31–32. (Professor Ian Haney López describes this form of political reaction as less a naturally occurring response to rapid social change than it is a strategic form of racism designed to maintain white supremacy when whites perceive advancement of the status of nonwhites.)

390 Kotlowski, *Nixon's Civil Rights: Politics, Principle, & Policy*, 117.

391 *DeFunis v. Odegaard*, 82 Wash. 2d 11, 21 (1973).

not equality and anti-discrimination, but diversity. Harvard sought a diverse student body for the benefit of all students and the institution itself. A goal of a diverse learning environment would keep preferences for legacy students, artists, athletes, and minority students intact. This argument caught the eye of Justice Powell, who would adopt it four years later in the transformative *Bakke* case.[392]

Decided in 1978, *Bakke* was the second affirmative action case to reach the Supreme Court. Allan Bakke, a white applicant to UC Davis Medical School, challenged a policy that reserved up to 16 of the school's 100 spots for minority and disadvantaged applicants. In a divided decision (4-4-1), the Supreme Court struck down the medical school's plan to the extent that it used quotas, while permitting the use of race as a factor in efforts to create a diverse student body. Justice Powell's opinion, which emphasized the value of diversity and the importance of a university's academic freedom to select its students, has endured as the framework for all subsequent affirmative action in U.S. higher education decisions. Justice Powell agreed with the four most conservative members of the Court that racial quotas were improper but was joined by the four more liberal members for the holding that race can be considered to promote diversity. His opinion adopts the argument advanced by Cox in the Harvard College amicus brief in *DeFunis*. After *Bakke*, affirmative action in U.S. higher education is acceptable where race is used as one of many factors considered in admissions, in order to create a diverse student body. Within a decade, most colleges in the U.S. had adopted admission policies allowing them to take race, ethnicity, and other factors into account in order to admit a diverse student body.[393]

Under the conservative portion of the *Bakke* decision, and the cases that followed, any state decision that uses race or national origin as a metric, whether "discriminatory" or "benign," is subjected to the Court's strictest standard of review. A state actor must have a "compelling interest" that is "narrowly tailored" to achieve that objective in order to be valid. A college or university's interest in providing diversity is regarded as sufficiently compelling to justify the use of race, but no other justification has been accepted.

---

392 Oppenheimer, "Archibald Cox and the Diversity Justification for Affirmative Action," 160–162.

393 Brief of Harvard University, Brown University, The University of Chicago, Dartmouth College, Duke University, The University of Pennsylvania, Princeton University, and Yale University as Amici Curiae Supporting Respondents, *Grutter v. Bollinger*, 2003 WL 399220, *8 (U.S. Feb. 8, 2003).

Twenty-five years after the *Bakke* case, the Supreme Court took up two University of Michigan affirmative action cases. In *Gratz v. Bollinger*, the Court (in a 5-4 decision) struck down the University's undergraduate affirmative action program, in which students were admitted on a point system, with a specified number of points given for being a member of a minority race.[394] The Court deemed this policy too similar to a numerical quota system.[395]

However, in *Grutter v. Bollinger*, the Court (again in a 5-4 decision, with Justice O'Connor creating a majority in each case) reaffirmed the Powell opinion in *Bakke*. The University of Michigan's law school program used a "holistic" review of application material, in which an applicant's membership in a minority race was a "plus" factor. The plan was modeled after Harvard's plan and sought to enroll a 'critical mass' of minority students in order to avoid isolation in the classroom.[396] Critically, the Court embraced the "critical mass theory," as first suggested in the Cox/Harvard brief in *DeFunis*, which argued that a diversity policy must pay attention to numerical goals to ensure that Black or other minority students be sufficiently well represented in the student body that they not be racially isolated.[397]

In 2013 and again in 2016, the University of Texas' affirmative action plan was reviewed by the Supreme Court and upheld as legitimate.[398] UT Austin admits seventy-five percent of its students through automatic admission to students graduating in the top ten percent of their high school (the "Texas 10% plan"). Because Texas remains so residentially segregated, the plan operated as a "facially neutral" alternative to selecting minority students based on their race.[399] But one effect of the plan was that Black and Latinx students from the State's few integrated school districts were often excluded, although they were well qualified and would increase the university's diversity. The University thus supplemented the 10% plan with a Harvard-like affirmative action plan to admit the remaining twenty-five percent of its students. Abigail Fisher, a white student not in the top ten percent of her high school class, challenged the latter plan. In *Fisher I* (another 5-4 decision), the court held that a diversity

394 *Gratz v. Bollinger*, 539 U.S. 244, 275–276 (2003).

395 Ibid. at 272–275.

396 *Grutter v. Bollinger*, 539 U.S. 306, 341–344 (2003).

397 Ibid. (writing for the court Justice O'Connor endorsed the critical mass theory of diversity-based admissions); *See also* Oppenheimer, "Archibald Cox and the Diversity Justification for Affirmative Action," 161–167.

398 *Fisher v. University of Texas at Austin*, 133 S. Ct. 2411 (*Fisher I*) (2013); *Fisher v. University of Texas at Austin*, 136 S. Ct. 2198 (*Fisher II*) (2016).

399 *Fisher*, 133 S. Ct., at 2431–2434. (*But see* dissenting opinion of Justice Ginsburg, arguing that the 10% plan is not "race blind;" it merely reflects the de-facto racial housing segregation throughout the State, thereby insuring that in any high school the top students will reflect the race of the school's effectively segregated student body.)

justification must be examined in order to determine if there are race blind policies that would have a similar impact. In *Fisher II* the court held that the school properly determined that there were not any race blind alternatives, and the Texas plan was a legitimate program for increasing the number of minority students. The court re-affirmed the *Bakke* decision based on the importance of diversity, once again in a 5-4 decision.[400]

While the diversity justification for affirmative action in higher education is by now well-established, positive measures aimed at integration of white and minority students in primary and secondary schools are nonetheless regarded as Constitutionally suspect. In *Parents Involved in Community Schools v. Seattle School District No. 1*, (2007) the Supreme Court held that the Seattle school district had violated the 14th Amendment [Equal Protection] rights of its students by assigning them to schools based on their race. Race had been considered as a factor in school assignment to avoid re-segregation of the schools.[401] Writing for the 5-4 majority, Chief Justice Roberts found that using race to prevent segregation was no different than the Jim Crow practices of using race to require segregation, exclaiming, "the way to end discrimination is to stop discriminating."[402]

Despite the Supreme Court's opinions upholding affirmative action in higher education, it remains controversial. In 1980, Ronald Reagan made opposition to affirmative action a centerpiece in his Presidential campaign.[403] In a number of states including California, Washington, and Michigan, the voters have amended either their state constitutions or civil rights statutes to prohibit affirmative action.[404] In California, the number of Black students at the University of California's Berkeley and Los Angeles campuses dropped dramatically with the 1996 passage of the voter initiative that prohibits affirmative action, and remains substantially below where it was prior to 1996.[405]

---

400 *Fisher*, 136 S. Ct. at 2214.

401 *Parents*, 551 U.S. at 709–714.

402 Ibid.

403 Parikh, *The Politics of Preference: Democratic Institutions and Affirmative Action in the United States and India*, 128; Denise M. Bostdorff and Steven R. Goldzwig, "History, Collective Memory, and the Appropriation of Martin Luther King, Jr.: Reagan's Rhetorical Legacy," *Presidential Studies Quarterly* 35, no. 4 (December 2005): 674–677.

404 CAL. CONST., art. I, § 31 (added by Initiative Measure Prop. 209, approved Nov. 5, 1996, eff. Nov. 6, 1996); WASH. REV. CODE § 49.60.400 (enacted by Initiative Measure No. 200, approved November 3, 1998); MICH. CONST., art. I, § 26 (enactment ratified Nov. 7, 2006, eff. Dec. 23, 2006).

405 David B. Oppenheimer, "Color-Blindness, Racism-Blindness, and Racism-Awareness: Revisiting Judge Henderson's Proposition 209 Decision," *Berkeley Journal of African American Law & Policy* 12 (2011): 243.

Some argue that affirmative action should be based on class and geography, not race or ethnicity.[406] In my recent paper reviewing Dr. Martin Luther King's views of affirmative action, I argue that race and class-based affirmative action should be complementary rather than mutually exclusive.[407]

Recently, critics of affirmative action have brought high-profile cases against Harvard and the University of North Carolina challenging their use of race in admissions, for which there have been expressions of support from the Trump administration.[408] Their argument is that diversity policies discriminate against Asian-American applicants, and that the proper remedy is to end affirmative action for Black and Latinx applicants.

2.2 *Positive Measures in Higher Education in India*

As described in the employment/labor law section, in pre-colonial times India was governed through a compartmentalized hierarchy, or caste system, in which lower caste Indians, including those in the lowest caste group formerly known as the "Harijans" or "Dalits," (or the now disfavored term "untouchables,") were disadvantaged in every area of life.[409]

During the British Colonial period in India, British rulers largely embraced the traditional caste system as a mechanism of control. Admission to schools was particularly difficult for lower caste Indians. Though in 1858 the Colonial government reserved the right to refuse support to schools that excluded students on account of caste or race, Galanter reports that opposition from higher castes was so strong that the Department of Public Instruction could "do very little in the matter."[410]

Anti-caste movements beginning in the mid-1800s supported some forms of preferential treatment for "untouchable" castes.[411] Most reform movements were self-organized, with an initial focus on allowing a process of upgrading

---

406 *See e.g.*, Tomiko Brown-Nagin, "Rethinking Proxies for Disadvantage in Higher Education: A First Generation Students' Project," *University of Chicago Legal Forum* 1 (2014): 433; contra Khiara M. Bridges, "The Deserving Poor, the Undeserving Poor, and Class-Based Affirmative Action," *Emory Law Journal* 66 (2017): 1101.

407 Oppenheimer, "Dr. King's Dream of Affirmative Action," 59–60.

408 *See generally Students for Fair Admissions, Inc. v. President & Fellows of Harvard Coll.* (Harvard Corp.), 308 F.R.D. 39 (D. Mass. 2015); *see also generally Students for Fair Admissions, Inc. v. University of North Carolina*, No. 1:14-cv-00954 (D.M.D.N.C. filed Nov. 17, 2014); Charlie Savage, "Justice Dept. to Take on Affirmative Action in College Admissions," accessed August 1, 2017. https://www.nytimes.com/2017/08/01/us/politics/trump-affirmative-action-universities.html.

409 Deshpande, *Affirmative Action in India*, 11–12.

410 Galanter, *Competing Equalities: Law and the Backward Classes in India*, 22.

411 Deshpande, *Affirmative Action in India*, 45–46.

caste status. Eventually reformers turned toward seeking political representation, government jobs, and scholarships.[412] Activists Jyotiba and Savitribai Phule, themselves members of the Shudra caste (a relatively low caste, but above the Dalits), were particularly influential in leading anti-caste movements in education.[413] Some scholars consider their work the catalyst to applying the necessary pressure on the colonial government to, at least officially, allow low-caste students into government-run schools.[414]

Quotas were introduced as part of the colonial policy of permitting various groups to have a voice within the limited self-government permitted under colonial rule. By independence, India had a history of reservations defined by caste for civil service positions and other benefits, including places in colleges.[415] As with reservations in employment, the first spots were reserved under Shahu's 50% reservations for "untouchables" in 1902, but the current form of affirmative action in India originates in the fight against Brahmin dominance in education which culminated in reservations for all non-Brahmin castes in both education and state services.[416]

Upon gaining its independence, India wrote affirmative action reservations into its 1948 Constitution. These policies reserved places for public employment and admission to public universities for the lower castes and for non-Hindus based on a formula intended to provide equal opportunity both in law and in fact.[417]

An explicit constitutional basis for educational reservations was added to the constitution in 1951. This was in response to the Indian Supreme Court judgment in *State of Madras v. Dorairajan*,[418] which found that a caste quota at a medical school violated Article 29[2] of the Constitution. Article 29[2] provides that no student shall be denied admission on ground of caste. In *Dorairajan*, a medical school adopted quotas to promote the admission of religious minorities and lower castes, in order to ensure an entering class with

412 Galanter, *Competing Equalities: Law and the Backward Classes in India*, 23–24; Krishnan and Devi, *A Crusade for Social Justice; Bending Governance towards the Deprived*, 169.

413 Deshpande, *Affirmative Action in India*, 45–46.

414 Balaji Pandey, "Educational Development among Scheduled Castes," *Social Scientist* 14, no. 2/3 (1986): 59.

415 Deshpande, *Affirmative Action in India*, 49–53; Galanter, *Competing Equalities: Law and the Backward Classes in India*, 27.

416 Deshpande, *Affirmative Action in India*, 49–53; Galanter, *Competing Equalities: Law and the Backward Classes in India*, 27; "Life History of Shahu Chhatrapati."

417 Deshpande, *Affirmative Action in India*, 54–55.

418 *State of Madras v. Dorairajan*, AIR 1951 SC 226.

a demographic composition similar to that of the general population.[419] The Court ruled in favor of the high-caste Hindu who had challenged the rule after being denied admission.[420] In response, Parliament immediately invalidated the ruling by adding Article 15, Clause 4 of the Indian Constitution, which provides that state action to advance the interest of lower-caste citizens does not run afoul of the Constitution's other provisions against discrimination.[421]

Positive measures in higher education are implemented in three basic types.[422] There are (1) quotas for university admissions, (2) fee concessions, scholarships, or grants, and (3) reduced minimum qualifying marks for admission. The system providing for quotas for university admissions has been the most controversial.[423]

The government's continued justification for reservation policies is that the framers of the Constitution thought that "mere anti-discrimination provisions could only guarantee a formal equality that would not be effective in combating the historically entrenched inequality. Resources are unequally distributed, and social customs are set in a hierarchical mode. The 'right to equality, whether equal protection of the laws or equality of opportunity, would have little security without important changes in the [social] structure of [Indian] society.'"[424]

A series of Supreme Court decisions beginning in the 1990s have reaffirmed the Indian commitment to positive measures in higher education through reservations. In *Sawhney v. Union of India* (1993),[425] the Court concluded that reservations in favor of the backward classes are permissible under the Indian Constitution; that reservations should generally be limited to fifty percent; that classification should be based on degrees of social backwardness; that wealthy members of a backward class (the "creamy layer") should be excluded from reservations; that reservations should be limited to appointments, and should not be used for promotion; and that the Government should appoint a

419 Clark D. Cunningham, "Affirmative Action: India's Example," *Civil Rights Journal*, (Fall 1999): 23.

420 Ibid.

421 Ibid.; CONSTITUTION OF INDIA, art. 15, § 4.

422 Galanter, *Competing Equalities: Law and the Backward Classes in India*, 43.

423 Brown and Sitapati, "Lessons Learned from Comparing the Application of Constitutional Law and Federal Anti-Discrimination Law to African-Americans in the U.S. and Dalits in India in the Context of Higher Education," 44 (noting that it is likely many of the reserved spots remain unfilled).

424 Ibid. at 21.

425 *Sawhney* AIR 1993 SC 477 at para 86.

permanent body to determine lists of backward classes.[426] The decision relies on a theory of substantive, rather than formal equality: "Among others, the concept of equality before the law contemplates minimizing the inequalities in income and eliminating the inequalities in status, facilities and opportunities not only amongst individuals but also amongst groups of people, securing adequate means of livelihood to its citizens and to promote with special care the education and economic interests of the weaker sections of the people, including in particular the Scheduled Castes and Scheduled Tribes and to protect them from social injustice and all forms of exploitation."[427] The "creamy layer" exception is grounded in the desire to ensure that "affirmative action is targeted only to [those who] suffer ... the greatest economic deprivation."[428]

Interestingly for those interested in comparative law, the *Sawhney* decision discusses at length the U.S. Supreme Court decision in *Regents of the University of California v. Bakke*, concluding that Justice Powell's diversity justification for affirmative action is less convincing than the equality arguments advanced by Justice Brennan. The Court found that the quest for equality was an independent and appropriate justification for reservations for minority students.[429]

In *Singh v. State of Bihar* (1994),[430] the Court upheld reservations in postgraduate medical courses.[431] The Court rejected the argument that reservations are "anti-meritarian," based on a belief that small concessions in admission standards do not lead to disparate performance throughout the education process. The Court relied in part on the fact that there are no "back-end" reservations, so all students must take, and pass or fail, the same final medical exams.[432]

In *Thakur v. Union of India*, (2008)[433] the Court re-affirmed reservations for socially and educationally disadvantaged classes (termed OBC – Other Backward Classes") in higher education placements, and re-affirmed that the "creamy layer" should be excluded. Here again, the Justices referenced U.S. Supreme Court holdings on affirmative action and other U.S. Supreme Court jurisprudence focusing on racial classifications.[434]

---

426 Ibid.

427 Ibid.

428 McCrudden, "A Comparative Taxonomy of 'Positive Action' and 'Affirmative Action' Policies," 14.

429 *Sawhney* AIR 1993 SC 477 at para 86.

430 *Singh v. State of Bihar*, 1994 SCC (4) 401, para 31.

431 Ibid. at para 5.

432 Ibid.

433 *Thakur*, 6 SCC 1, para 140.

434 Ibid. at para 11.

Beginning in 2006, upon enactment of the 93rd Amendment to the Indian Constitution,[435] reservations are available in both public and private institutions. However, that amendment is not self-executing; state and federal governments must pass legislation to implement it.[436]

The number of scheduled caste and OBC students who reached higher education increased steadily throughout second half of the Twentieth Century.[437] Yet reservation quotas are often left unimplemented or unfilled, and expenditures set aside for reservation programs are often not spent.[438] Brown and Sitapati observe that "whether Dalits actually occupy these reserved seats is difficult to determine. The government has compiled no countrywide statistics for higher education. Evidence collected from specific universities suggests that the number of reserved seats filled may only be about fifty percent."[439]

Despite the current system of reservations, India continues to confront substantial inequality and discrimination. Though contemporary India is committed by law to the idea of a classless society, disparities in the "standards of living, poverty rates, health status, educational attainment, and occupational outcomes"[440] between lower and upper caste citizens are striking. Individuals classified as Scheduled Castes and Tribes are twice as likely to be poor as those in higher castes.[441] The wage gap between the two categories was 0.61 as of 2009–2010.[442] Disparities in land ownership remain persistent.[443]

Members of the Dalit caste are still subject to stigmatization and exclusionary practices, particularly in rural India. Denial of housing, public accommodations, employment, and access to goods and services (including midwifery) is common.[444] Caste continues to be the strongest predictor of a student's likelihood to drop out or repeat a grade, and members of Scheduled Castes and Tribes are the lowest enrolled class in higher education.[445]

---

435 Constitution of India, amend. XCIII.

436 Brown and Sitapati, "Lessons Learned from Comparing the Application of Constitutional Law and Federal Anti-Discrimination Law to African-Americans in the U.S. and Dalits in India in the Context of Higher Education," 21.

437 Galanter, *Competing Equalities: Law and the Backward Classes in India*, 61–62.

438 Ibid. at 63–65.

439 Brown and Sitapati, "Lessons Learned from Comparing the Application of Constitutional Law and Federal Anti-Discrimination Law to African-Americans in the U.S. and Dalits in India in the Context of Higher Education," 44.

440 Deshpande, *Affirmative Action in India*, 21.

441 Ibid.

442 Ibid. at 22.

443 Ibid. at 24.

444 Ibid.

445 Galanter, *Competing Equalities: Law and the Backward Classes in India*, 60.

Meanwhile, critics of the reservations system regard them as polarizing.[446] They question whether disparities of opportunity are great enough to justify the reservations and argue that the data supporting reservations is suspect because when caste was abolished in the constitution, it was also removed as a category in the census.[447] Critics also ask whether 'backwardness' should be defined in terms of class, income, or religion,[448] and assert that reservations are anti-meritocratic and therefore fundamentally unfair.[449]

Recently the Indian lower house passed a bill establishing a 10% educational reservation for "economically weaker sections."[450] This suggests that India is also branching out to address economic inequality through educational reservations as well as the other forms of social inequality it seeks to combat.

2.3 *Positive Measures in Higher Education in Brazil*

As described in the employment section, Brazil was the largest importer of African slaves in the world.[451] As a result, most living Brazilians are descendants of the three-racial/ethnic groups who populated Brazil during colonial times – Portuguese colonialist, indigenous people, and African slaves.[452] Although Brazil has high rates of so-called "miscegenation," Brazilian society has a clear racial hierarchy.[453] The racial divide is especially notable in the education, media, and employment sectors.[454] People who identify as white are at the top of the socio-economic hierarchy.[455] Racially-mixed individuals fall just below, while Afro-Brazilians remain at the bottom of the hierarchy.[456] Darker skinned Brazilians are associated with the lower class, have less access

446 Deshpande, *Affirmative Action in India*, 6–7.

447 Parikh, *The Politics of Preference: Democratic Institutions and Affirmative Action in the United States and India*, 165.

448 Deshpande, *Affirmative Action in India*, 6–7.

449 Ibid.

450 Ministry of Social Justice and Empowerment, *The Constitution (One Hundred and Twenty Fourth Amendment) Bill, 2019*. New Delhi: PRS Legislative Research, 2019. Accessed February 22, 2019. https://www.prsindia.org/billtrack/constitution-one-hundred-and-twenty-fourth-amendment-bill-2019.

451 Johnson III and Heringer, *Race, Politics, and Education in Brazil*, 1.

452 Stanley R. Bailey, *Legacies of Race Identities, Attitudes, and Policies in Brazil* (Stanford: Stanford University Press, 2009): 1.

453 Martins, Medeiros and Nascimento, "Paving Paradise: the Road from "Racial Democracy" to Affirmative Action in Brazil," 809.

454 Htun, "From 'Racial Democracy' to Affirmative Action: Changing State Policy on Race in Brazil," 74. https://doi.org/10.1353/lar.2004.0010.

455 Ibid. at 62; Bernardino-Costa and Blackman, "Affirmative Action in Brazil," 374.

456 Htun, "Racial Democracy," 62; Bernardino-Costa and Blackman, "Affirmative Action in Brazil," 374.

to education, and generally hold less prestigious jobs.[457] Whiteness, on the other hand, is correlated with money, higher education, and better employment opportunities.[458] Rafael Guerreiro Osorio writes, "As Brazil has been a very unequal society throughout its history, those at the bottom have always been far below those at the top – the descendents of the European colonisers."[459]

While Brazil has had a constitutional commitment to equality since 1934, there was negligible movement towards turning that into meaningful action to promote substantive equality until toward the end of the 1990s, when the Brazilian government began introducing measures recognizing the lasting effects racism has had on Afro-Brazilian people.[460] A 1995 legislative proposal, Bill of Law 14/95, called for a quota system for higher education institutions.[461] The Bill was never voted on, but it introduced the idea of affirmative action to the Brazilian legislature.[462]

In 2001, Rio de Janeiro's State Legislative Assembly approved Law 3708, which introduced a quota system for the State University of Rio de Janeiro and the State University of North Fluminense.[463] The law required the designated universities to reserve 40% of the seats for Afro-Brazilian, racially-mixed, and indigenous students.[464]

In 2003, after much public critique, Rio de Janeiro's State Legislative Assembly reduced the quota percentage by requiring 20% of the seats be reserved for students from public schools and another 20% for Afro-Brazilian students.[465] Many other Brazilian universities followed suit, but racial quotas in universities are still subject to public debate among Brazilians.[466]

In 2012, the Brazilian Federal Supreme Court upheld the constitutionality and legality of affirmative action programs.[467] In the opinion, Justice Joaquim

457 Htun, "Racial Democracy," 74.

458 Ibid.

459 Rafael Guerreiro Osorio, "The Persistence of Black-White Income Differentials in Brazil," in *Affirmative Action in Plural Societies: International Experiences*, eds. Graham K. Brown, Arnim Langer, and Frances Stewart (New York: Palgrave Macmillan, 2012): 119.

460 Dischino, "Affirmative Action in Brazil: Reverse Discrimination and the Creation of a Constitutionally Protected Color-Line," 170; Constituicao Federal [C.F.] [Constitution] art. 113, § 1 (1934); *See also* Bernardino-Costa and Blackman, "Affirmative Action in Brazil," 374.

461 Martins, Medeiros, and Nascimento, "Paving Paradise," 798.

462 Ibid.

463 Bernardino-Costa and Blackman, "Affirmative Action in Brazil," 375.

464 Ibid.

465 Ibid. at 376; Martins, Medeiros, and Nascimento, "Paving Paradise," 809.

466 Bernardino-Costa and Blackman, "Affirmative Action in Brazil," 376–379.

467 Rubia R. Valente and Brian J. Berry, "Performance of Students Admitted through Affirmative Action in Brazil," *Latin American Research Review* 52, no. 1 (2017): 20.

Barbosa wrote, "Affirmative Actions are defined as public policies directed to fulfill the constitutional principles of material equality and to neutralize the pervasive effects of discrimination of race, gender, age, national origin or disability … These measures aim to fight not only flagrant manifestations of discrimination, but de facto discrimination, that is so absolutely rooted in our society, so well rooted, that [most] people do not perceive it."[468]

In 2012, President Rousseff signed a law requiring 50% of the seats in federal universities be reserved for students from public high schools.[469] In addition, the law requires a proportional percentage of the seats be reserved for "black, brown, and indigenous students," according to the racial proportions of the city where the university is located.[470] As of 2015, 80% of state universities and 100% of federal universities have some form of affirmative action policy in place.[471] Some quota policies reserve slots only for students from public high schools.[472] Other affirmative action programs consider only race or a combination of both.[473]

Brazilian society's reaction to affirmative action policies has been controversial. Mala Htun observes that some Brazilians are "hostile to challenges to the racial democracy thesis and reluctant to admit to racism."[474] Critics of affirmative action claim it is too difficult to define whom the beneficiaries should be,[475] because Brazil's high rates of so-called "miscegenation" make it difficult to define who is Black.[476] Some critics fear that individuals will self-identify as Afro-Brazilian only to benefit from the quota systems.[477] Some argue that quotas will lead to reverse racism.[478]

As described in the employment section, in October 2018 Brazil elected Jair Bolsonaro President.[479] He is an opponent of affirmative action and has

---

468 As quoted in, Valente and Berry, "Performance of Students," 20; Supremo Tribunal Federal (Federal Supreme Court of Brazil). *Press Release University of Brasilia Affirmative Action Case, Docket No. ADPF 186*. April 26, 2012.

469 Valente and Berry, "Performance of Students," 21.

470 Ibid.

471 Johnson and Heringer, "Race, Politics, and Education," 189.

472 Valente and Berry, "Performance of Students," 21.

473 Ibid.

474 Htun, "Racial Democracy," 61.

475 Martins, Medeiros, and Nascimento, "Paving Paradise," 809.

476 Ibid.

477 Ibid. at 810.

478 Htun, "Racial Democracy," 73.

479 Ernesto Londoño, and Shasta Darlington, "Jair Bolsonaro Wins Brazil's Presidency, in a Shift to the Far Right," *The New York Times*. October 28, 2018, accessed February 3, 2019. https://www.nytimes.com/2018/10/28/world/americas/jair-bolsonaro-brazil-election.html.

promised to reduce it.[480] In addition to seeking to reduce affirmative action there are fears that President Bolsonaro may seek to make education in Brazil less inclusive for LGBTQ individuals, given that a major plank of his campaign was to reverse an alleged LGBTQ agenda in public education.[481]

2.4 *Positive Measures in Higher Education in South Africa*

Under the Apartheid system, from 1948 to 1994 South Africa was rigidly segregated, and educational opportunity for Black South Africans varied from nonexistent to extremely limited.[482] The 1950 School Board Acts instituted government schools for White students only.[483] The Bantu Education Act of 1953 permitted Black education but required the segregation of universities and schools by race and tribe.[484] The Government emphasized schools focusing on low-paying trade and labor jobs for Black South Africans.[485] As described in the Employment/Labor section, in 1994, South Africa adopted a democratic government committed to addressing the racial disparities created by apartheid, especially in the education sector.[486]

As described in the employment section, the positive legal justification for post-apartheid affirmative action in education as well as employment is found in Section 9 of the South African Constitution,[487] which explicitly provides

480 *See* Ciara Nugent, "How Far-Right Populist Jair Bolsonaro Could Transform Brazil," *Time*. October 25, 2018, accessed February 3, 2019. http://time.com/5433379/brazil-bolsonaro-policies/; David Biller, "Bolsonaro Says Black Brazilians Aren't Owed Anything Over Slavery," *Bloomberg.com*. July 31, 2018, accessed February 3, 2019. https://www.bloomberg.com/news/articles/2018-07-31/brazil-candidate-bolsonaro-minimizes-slavery-praises-trump.

481 Zoe Sullivan, "'We're Afraid': Advocates Say Brazil's Presidential Frontrunner a Threat to Gay Rights," *NBCNews.com*. October 6, 2018, accessed February 3, 2019. https://www.nbcnews.com/feature/nbc-out/we-re-afraid-advocates-say-brazil-s-presidential-frontrunner-threat-n917111.

482 Uduak Archibong and Oluyinka Adejumo, "Affirmative Action in South Africa: Are we Creating New Casualties?," *Journal of Psycological Issues in Organizational Culture* 3, no. S1 (2013): 14; Judith February, "From Redress to Empowerment: The New South African Constitution and Its Implementation," in *The Next Twenty-Five Years: Affirmative Action in Higher Education in the United States and South Africa*, eds. David L. Featherman, Marvin Krislov, and Martin Hall (Ann Arbor: University of Michigan Press, 2010), 81.

483 Beverly Lindsay, "Toward Conceptual, Policy, and Programmatic Frameworks of Affirmative Action in South African Universities," *The Journal of Negro Education* 66, no. 4 (Autumn, 1997): 523.

484 February, "From Redress to Empowerment," 81.

485 Ibid.

486 Saleem Badat and YuSuf Sayed, "Post-1994 South African Education: The Challenge of Social Justice," *The Annals of the American Academy* 652 (March 2014): 129.

487 S. Afr. Const., 1996, Section 9.

for positive action and embraces a substantive model of equality, rejecting a formal equality model by only prohibiting *unfair* discrimination:[488]

> (1) Everyone is equal before the law and has the right to equal protection and benefit of the law. (2) Equality includes the full and equal enjoyment of all rights and freedoms. To promote the achievement of equality, legislative and other measures designed to protect or advance persons, or categories of persons, disadvantaged by unfair discrimination may be taken. (3) The state may not unfairly discriminate directly or indirectly against anyone on one or more grounds, including race, gender, sex, pregnancy, marital status, ethnic or social origin, colour, sexual orientation, age, disability, religion, conscience, belief, culture, language and birth. (4) No person may unfairly discriminate directly or indirectly against anyone on one or more grounds in terms of subsection (3). National legislation must be enacted to prevent or prohibit unfair discrimination. (5) Discrimination on one or more of the grounds listed in subsection (3) is unfair unless it is established that the discrimination is fair.[489]

This in turn provides the constitutional basis for not only South Africa's anti-discrimination policies, but also for the country's affirmative action policies.

Accordingly, in light of the constitutional permissiveness of affirmative action and the deep inequality present in South African society, between 1994 and 2013 the government adopted several legislative measures and studies regarding affirmative action policies.[490] This included: Seven white papers, three green paper, 26 Bills, 35 Acts, 11 regulations, 52 government notices, and 26 calls for comments.[491] The 1995 White Paper on Education and Training called upon States to remedy the educational inequalities for disadvantaged individuals in order to equalize learning opportunities.[492] The National Education Policy

---

488 Ibid. at 5–6.

489 Ibid.

490 YuSuf Sayed, Anil Kanjee, Mokubung Nkomo, *The Search for Education Quality in Post-Apartheid South Africa: Interventions to Improve Learning and Teaching* (Cape Town: HSRC Press, May 2013), 5–38.

491 Ibid.

492 Badat and Sayed, "Post-1994," 129; *see also* Department of Education, *White Paper on Education & Training*, Cape Town: Department of Education, 1995. Accessed Feb. 14, 2018. https://www.education.gov.za/Portals/0/Documents/Legislation/White%20paper/White%20paper%20on%20Education%20and%20Training%201995.pdf?ver=2008-03-05-111656-000.

Act 27 of 1996 adopted a policy of "democratic transformation of the national system of education into one which serves the needs and interest of all of the people of South Africa and upholds their fundamental rights."[493] The Higher Education Act of 1997 required universities to develop "appropriate measures for the redress of past inequalities,"[494] including affirmative action policies.[495]

Although South Africa's higher education affirmative action policies have been controversial, there have been only a handful of court challenges. In an early case, *Motala v. University of Natal*, a highly qualified candidate of Indian descent was denied admission to the University of Natal's medical school program.[496] The University had a policy that only allowed the acceptance of 40 Indian students per class, thus reserving seats for Black, Colored, and white students. The applicant's parents filed a claim that the policy limiting the number of Indian students was racially discriminatory and violated the South African Constitution. The court agreed that the University's procedure assessed African applicants differently than Indian applicants but held that the policy's goal to protect and advance a disadvantaged group of people was allowed under section 8(3)(a) of the South African Constitution. The court reasoned that the disadvantages suffered by African students was "significantly greater than that suffered by their Indian counterparts." Therefore, the University's policy did not violate the South African Constitution.

Similarly, in *Rugnath v. University of Cape Town* (*UCT*) an Indian applicant was denied admission to the University of Cape Town School of Medicine. The applicant brought a claim against the school contending that the denial of admission constituted unfair racial discrimination. UCT acknowledged that its affirmative action admission policy was prima facie discriminatory but justified such discrimination as necessary to remedy past racial inequalities. The court held that the Higher Education Act allows universities to create their own admission standards so long as it redresses past inequalities in a fair and nondiscriminatory manner.[497]

493 National Education Policy Act 27 of 1996, preamble (S. Afr). http://www.puk.ac.za/opencms/export/PUK/html/fakulteite/opvoed/mediasentrum/Dokumente/godsdiensonderwysbeleid.pdf.

494 February, "From Redress to Empowerment," 77.

495 Ibid.

496 *Motala and Another v. University of Natal* 1995 (3) BCLR 374 (D), at 11–14.

497 High Court of South Africa. *In the High Court of South Africa (Cape of Good Hope Provincial Division), Cape Town: Tuesday 1 March 2005, Third Division: Court No. 16*. Cape Town: High Court of South Africa, 2005. Accessed February 10, 2018. https://www.westerncape.gov.za/other/2005/3/high_court_roll_1-4march05.pdf; February, "From Redress to Empowerment," 80.

In 1993, 70% of white South Africans attended some form of higher education as opposed to only 12% of Black South Africans.[498] According to a report commissioned by the Council on Higher Education, "higher education has made progress in changing the demographics of postgraduate enrolment and graduations in relation to both race and gender … the number of enrolments at postgraduate level has increased considerably since 1995."[499] Black student enrollment in all levels of higher education increased between 2000 and 2005.[500] Still, African first-enrollments have the lowest participation rates in master's and doctoral graduate programs when compared to their Indian and White counterparts.[501] "Whites in the age group 25–34 are 28 times more likely than their African counterparts to engage in and complete Doctoral studies in South Africa."[502]

2.5 *Positive Measures in Higher Education in France*

France provides an interesting example of a society that recognizes the problem of racism but declines to recognize the existence of race, not only as a biological, but also as a sociological construct or form of identity.[503] Saran Donahoo writes, "French Republicanism creates forced homogeneity by casting all inhabitants as French, while also denying the heterogeneous elements that exist within French culture … individual differences do not matter because *all* are French."[504] French law and social convention does not recognize racial minority statuses.[505]

---

498 Katherine C. Naff and Frederik Uys, "Representative Bureaucracy in South Africa: Success or Failure," (Paper presented to the annual meeting of the Midwest Political Science Association, April 7–10, 2005, Chicago).

499 The Council on Higher Education, "Postgraduate Studies in South Africa: A Statistical Profile." *Higher Education Monitor*, no. 7 (March 2009): vii. http://www.che.ac.za/sites/default/files/publications/CHE_MonitorProjectV7.pdf.

500 Ibid. at 26. (The study uses the term "Black" to refer to African, Coloured and Indian students).

501 Ibid. at xxiii.

502 Ibid. at xxiv.

503 John D. Skrentny, ed., *Color Lines: Affirmative Action, Immigration, and Civil Rights Options for America* (Chicago and London: The University of Chicago Press, 2001): 270.

504 Saran Donahoo, "Reflections on Race: Affirmative Action Policies Influencing Higher Education in France and the United States," *Teachers College Record* 110, no. 2 (February 2008): 254; *See also* Michael Banton, "National Integration in France and Britain," *Journal of Ethnic and Migration Studies* 27, no. 1 (2001): 166. doi:10.1080/13691830124752; Marilyn Osborn, Patricia Broadfoot, Claire Planel, and Andrew Pollard, "Social Class, Educational Opportunity and Equal Entitlement: Dilemmas of Schooling in England and France," *Comparative Education* 33, no. 3 (1997): 375–393.

505 Skrentny, *Color Lines*, 270; Déclaration du 26 août 1789 des droits de l'homme et du citoyen, [French Declaration of Human and Civic Rights], CONSEIL CONSTITUTIONNEL [CONSTITUTIONAL COUNCIL], Aug. 26, 1789; CONST (Fr.).

The French Declaration of Human and Civic Rights – adopted in 1789 by the French National Assembly – forms the first articles of the current French Constitution.[506] "Men are born and remain free and equal in rights" (Article 1).[507] "Law must be the same for all, both when it protects and punishes. All citizens being equal before the law, they shall have equal access to all honors, public positions and employments, depending on their merits and without other distinctions than those resulting from their virtues and talents" (Article 6).

These provisions are interpreted to require formal equality in all state action. French data protection law does not allow the "recording or storage in a computer memory of personal data which directly or indirectly reflect racial origins or political, philosophical, or religious opinions."[508] On November 15, 2007, the Constitutional Council held that collecting ethnic or racial origins in data collection processing violates Article 1 of the French Constitution,[509] even if the purpose is to measure discrimination.[510] Critics have countered, "if you're not counted, you don't count."[511] Given this commitment to formal equality, France is not a likely setting for affirmative action policies based on race or ethnicity. But for the past twenty years, France has engaged in an interesting experiment in admitting students from poor neighborhoods, most of whom are members of racial/ethnic minorities, into selective elite universities.

Because of France's unified education system, the government requires that all students follow the same curriculum regardless of the institution.[512] The French state, through the Ministry of Youth, Education, and Research, sets the unified education policy for France.[513] In light of this, Patrick Clancy and Gaële Goastellec observe that the French system for selecting students for the top universities operates, in effect, as a sorting device for the wealthy

506 Déclaration du 26 août 1789 des droits de l'homme et du citoyen, [French Declaration of Human and Civic Rights], CONSEIL CONSTITUTIONNEL [CONSTITUTIONAL COUNCIL], Aug. 26, 1789; CONST (Fr.).

507 Ibid.

508 Banton, "National Integration," 152.

509 The Constitutional Council. *Decision No. 2007-557 DC November 15th 2007*. Paris: The Constitutional Council, 2017. https://law.yale.edu/system/files/documents/pdf/Intellectual_Life/Decision_No.2007-557_DC_November_15th_2007.pdf.

510 Ibid.

511 Patrick Lozes, Interview with David B. Oppenheimer, Personal Interview, Paris: France, March 28, 2014. *See* Voice Of America, "Survey: Blacks in France Say They Face Racial Discrimination," *VOA*. November 1, 2009, accessed February 16, 2019. https://www.voanews.com/a/a-13-2007-02-05-voa27/404117.html.

512 Donahoo, "Reflections on Race," 257.

513 Ibid. at 256.

and the upper middle class.[514] This is because the French government is hesitant to recognize identities other than professional categories and as most universities are required to follow suit it is only "within the selective sector, the *Grandes Ecoles*, which have more autonomy than the universities, that we find some initiatives designed to achieve equality of opportunity."[515] The *Grandes Écoles* are specialized schools offering training in a limited number of subjects: including "science, mechanics, and military applications; business and commerce studies; architecture; law and civil administration; and miscellaneous institutions, such as those providing instruction in veterinary surgery, journalism, or translation."[516] One of the most prestigious institutions is the Institute for the Study of Political Science of Paris (widely described as "Sciences Po,") which focuses on national and international studies for students entering business, politics, law, or civil services.[517] Entrance into Sciences Po and the other *Grandes Écoles* is competitive and difficult but carries great prestige and helps move students up the social, political, and economic ladder.[518]

In 1998, a study by Madani Cheurfa and Vincent Tiberj on admissions data showed that 81.5 % of Sciences Po students came from upper to upper-middle class families;[519] 53.5 % students had parents employed in upper-level management or academics; 28% of students had parents who worked as professionals or entrepreneurs; and <1% of students had parents from working class backgrounds.[520] As a result of the study, the then-Director of Sciences Po, Richard Descoings (with the backing of the government's education minister) created the *Conventions éducation prioritaire* (CEP, or Equal Opportunity and Diversity Program) in order to increase diversity among students.[521]

The program allowed for a "special admission track" for students from specified high schools in economically disadvantaged areas ("*zones d'education*

514 Patrick Clancy and Gaële Goastellec, "Exploring Access and Equity in Higher Education: Policy and Performance in a Comparative Perspective," *Higher Education Quarterly* 61, no. 2 (April 2007): 138.

515 Ibid. at 141.

516 Donahoo, "Reflections on Race," 258.

517 Ibid.

518 Ibid.

519 Sabbagh, Daniel. "Affirmative Action at Sciences Po," *French Politics, Culture & Society* 20, no. 3 (2002): 53. http://www.jstor.org.libproxy.berkeley.edu/stable/42843247; Original Source: Madani Cheurfa and Vincent Tiberj, "Le Concours d'entrée à Sciences Po: inégalités d'accès et inégalités sociales," in *Convention ZEP. L'Excellence dans la diversité – Communiqué de synthèse*, pp. 3–4 (Sciences Po document, on file with author, Daniel Sabbagh).

520 Sabbagh, "Affirmative Action," 53.

521 Sabbagh, "Affirmative Action," 53; Donahoo, "Reflections on Race," 265.

prioritaire").[522] Although these zones are identified as socioeconomically disadvantaged areas they also equated to what are described as primarily "immigrant" neighborhoods[523] (although "immigrant" itself is often a euphemism for persons of color, since the descendants of Africans, Middle Easterners, Basques, Arabs, Muslims, and Jews may be fourth generation French and still be commonly described as "immigrants").

In the traditional method, students are selected for Sciences Po based on their transcripts, an interview, and *le baccalauréat scores* (the academic qualification exam students take after high school).[524] In addition, students are required to take a competitive exam (*Le Concours*).[525] Preparation for the exam often involves taking expensive preparatory courses.[526]

Under the CEP program, in lieu of taking *Le Concours*, students from the specified high schools can write and defend two papers before teachers and administrators at their high schools.[527] The rationale for such a program is that the preparatory courses needed to prepare and ensure success on *Le Concours* are too expensive for students from poor neighborhoods.[528] The top candidates are invited to interview at Sciences Po.[529] Admitted students are eligible to receive financial aid and optional tutoring.[530]

As a result of the CEP program, students from minority neighborhoods receive additional opportunities to attend top universities, from which they otherwise are effectively excluded. The program at Sciences Po tends to primarily benefit students who identifying ethnically or culturally with Africa,[531] with 70% of students selected through the program identify as belonging to families who came from Africa.[532] Programs like CEP, along with the 2005 race riots in Paris, has pushed the French people to talk somewhat more openly about issues of race and inequality.[533] Following the CEP program's success, several other *Grandes Écoles* institutions enacted similar affirmative action programs

522 Sabbagh, "Affirmative Action," 53.
523 Clancy and Goastellec, "Exploring Access and Equity," 141; Donahoo, "Reflections on Race," 263.
524 Donahoo, "Reflections on Race," 263.
525 Elise S. Langan, "Assimilation and Affirmative Action in French Education Systems," *European Education* 40, no. 3 (2008): 54.
526 Langan, "Assimilation and Affirmative Action," 54.
527 Sabbagh, "Affirmative Action," 53.
528 Donahoo, "Reflections on Race," 263.
529 Sabbagh, "Affirmative Action," 53.
530 Ibid.
531 Donahoo, "Reflections on Race," 263.
532 Ibid. at 267.
533 Ibid. at 270.

to facilitate entrance for disadvantaged students.[534] However, these programs were on a smaller scale.[535]

In 2001, *Le Conseil Constitutionnel* (the Constitutional Council of the Republic of France, roughly equivalent to a constitutional high court) issued a decision regarding the statute amending the Education Code that allowed the Council Sciences Po to adopt the CEP program (to "determine conditions and procedures for admission to the Institute").[536] Such methods included policies to "ensure diversified recruitment among student(s)."[537] The Council held that the amendment was in conformity with the Constitution so long as the methods used rested on objective criteria guaranteed to respect the constitutional requirement of equal access to education.[538]

Also, in 2001, the National Interuniversity Union (UNI) requested the Court Tribunal of Paris declare the CEP program unconstitutional on the basis that the program gives special benefits to low-income students and violates the equal opportunity guarantees of the French Constitution.[539] On review by the Paris Administrative Appeals Court in 2003, the policy was upheld with some modifications.[540]

Critics argue that CEP goes against the French principles of equal treatment[541] and decreases the "commitment to intellectual merit and academic excellence" of France's prestigious institutions.[542] Critics also claim that CEP will affect the quality of training at Sciences Po[543] and that it too closely resembles "quotas and differential treatment," which goes against French principles.[544]

Proponents of CEP claim that it improves general educational achievements[545] and increases diversity, which will affect the future of

534 Agnes Zante, "Widening Participation in France and Its Effects on the Field of Elite Higher Education and on Educational Policy," in *Policy and Inequality in Education*, eds. Stephen Parker, Kalervo N. Gulson, and Trevor Gale, (Glasgow and Sydney: Springer, 2017), 79.

535 Ibid.

536 Conseil Constitutionnel [CC] [Constitutional Court] Decision No. 2001-450 cd.-July 11, 2001, J.O. 11506. https://www.conseil-constitutionnel.fr/decision/2001/2001450DC.htm.

537 Ibid.

538 Ibid.

539 Langan, "Assimilation and Affirmative Action," 57.

540 Ibid.; Sasha Polakow-Suransky, "CRÈME DE LA CRÈME," *Legal Affairs*. July/August 2004, accessed February 3, 2019. http://www.legalaffairs.org/issues/July-August-2004/story_suransky_julaug04.msp.

541 Sabbagh, "Affirmative Action," 54.

542 Donahoo, "Reflections on Race," 268.

543 Parker, Gulson, and Gale, *Policy and Inequality*, 79.

544 Langan, "Assimilation and Affirmative Action," 56.

545 Sabbagh, "Affirmative Action," 54.

France's leaders.[546] Proponents assert that Sciences Po's prestige has not decreased.[547] Institutions with affirmative action programs like CEP continue to maintain standards for academic excellence.[548] Donahoo observes that "students admitted via affirmative action programs tend to replicate the academic standards in place at the colleges and universities that they go on to attend."[549] CEP also encourages teachers serving in disadvantaged neighborhoods because they see more opportunity for students to attend prestigious universities.[550] Finally, CEP gives better access to good employment opportunities for students from disadvantaged backgrounds.[551]

2.6 *Positive Measures in Higher Education in China*

China, a nation of nearly 1.4 billion people, is largely controlled by the ethnic Han community, but includes substantial numbers of people identified as ethnic minorities, many of whom live in regions far from central China.[552] Sautman asserts that "like [W]hites in the United States, the majority Han are implicitly the standard by which all other groups are judged and usually not seen as 'ethnic.'"[553] The national minority groups tend to populate the poorest regions in China, resulting in low funding for schools and other economic needs.[554] Secondary schools tend to be the most well-resourced when located in urban centers, with few minority students.[555] As such, educational achievement gaps exist between the Han majority group and China's national minorities in a variety of dimensions and levels of education.[556]

546 Ibid.

547 Ibid.

548 Donahoo, "Reflections on Race," 268.

549 Ibid. at 270.

550 Parker, Gulson, and Gale, *Policy and Inequality*, 83.

551 Ibid.

552 Barry Sautman, "Affirmative Action, Ethnic Minorities and China's Universities," *Pacific Rim Law & Policy Journal* 7, no. 1 (1998): 80.

553 Ann Maxwell Hill and Minglang Zhou, "Introduction," in *Affirmative Action in China and the U.S.: A Dialogue on Inequality and Minority Education*, eds. Ann Maxwell Hill and Minlang Zhou (New York: Palgrave Macmillan, 2009), 5.

554 Gerard A. Postiglione, "China's National Minorities and Educational Change," *Journal of Contemporary Asia* 22, no. 1 (1992): 33; Tiezhi Wang, "Preferential Policies for Minority College Admission in China: Recent Developments, Necessity, and Impact," in *Affirmative Action in China and the U.S.: A Dialogue on Inequality and Minority Education*, ed. Ann Maxwell Hill and Minlang Zhou (New York: Palgrave MacMillan 2009), 75.

555 Wang, "Preferential Policies for Minority College Admission in China: Recent Developments, Necessity, and Impact," in Hill and Zhou, *Affirmative Action in China and the U.S.*, 76.

556 Postiglione, "China's National Minorities and Educational Change," 29.

In an effort to maintain or create a sense of a unified national identification across ethnic communities and integrate national minorities through education, China has a number of policies to recruit them into places of power, including quotas in recruitment and enrollment at top universities.[557]

Quotas have a long history in China. Ethnic minorities in China have been recruited for education in set numbers since the dynastic period. Dynasties ruled by the Han majority tended to use such positive measures in order to assimilate minorities into the mainstream culture.[558] During the Yuan and Qing dynasties, periods in which the Han were conquered and occupied, educational quotas for ethnic minorities were used to solidify the power of the ruling class.[559]

China's modern policies on positive action have their roots in seeking "one nation with diversity."[560] The Chinese Communist Party (CCP) developed some minority education policies before it came to power in 1949, even founding a college for Mongolian and Muslim students.[561] In the early Twenty-First Century, the CCP appears to have vacillated between a preferential treatment approach to minority students and one of formal equality among individuals rather than national groups.[562] Formally adopted in 1954, the first constitution of the People's Republic of China (PRC) endorsed equality for all national minorities, largely focusing on territorial autonomy.[563]

In 1950, the Chinese government published two documents, the *Preliminary Plan for the Training of Minority Cadres* and the *Preliminary Plan for the Founding of the Central Institute for Nationalities*. These documents laid the foundation for quotas, funding, organization, and the supervision of minority education.[564] Establishing these policies required identifying ethnic minorities that would be targeted for positive measures. From 1949–1979 the PRC identified and

---

557 Sautman, "Affirmative Action, Ethnic Minorities and China's Universities," 79; Postiglione, "China's National Minorities and Educational Change," 37; Hill and Zhou, "Introduction," in Hill and Zhou, *Affirmative Action in China and the U.S.*, 5.

558 Minglang Zhou, "Tracking the Historical Development of China's Positive and Preferential Policies for Minority Education: Continuities and Discontinuities," in *Affirmative Action in China and the U.S.: A Dialogue on Inequality and Minority Education*, ed. Ann Maxwell Hill and Minlang Zhou (New York: Palgrave Macmillan, 2009), 49–52.

559 Ibid.

560 Hill and Zhou, "Introduction," in Hill and Zhou, *Affirmative Action in China and the U.S.*, 5.

561 Zhou, "Tracking the Historical Development of China's Positive and Preferential Policies for Minority Education," in Hill and Zhou *Affirmative Action in China and the U.S.*, 55–57.

562 Ibid.

563 Hill and Zhou, "Introduction," in Hill and Zhou, *Affirmative Action in China and the U.S.*, 8.

564 Zhou, "Tracking the Historical Development of China's Positive and Preferential Policies for Minority Education," in Hill and Zhou *Affirmative Action in China and the U.S.*, 61.

classified minority communities into fifty-five groups.[565] State-sponsored preferential policies for ethnic minorities date back to this period but have been explicit PRC policy only since the mid-1980s–1990s.[566]

After the fall of the Soviet Union, the Chinese government immediately began to study the role of ethnic relations in the fall of the Soviet Union.[567] Findings included that minority republics could legally and easily secede from the Union, and that local minority control of government functions and a deeply depressed economy led minority communities to feel separated from the Union both in opportunity and in governance. These findings prompted further attention in developing a Chinese national identity through embracing the country's diversity.[568] "The concept of diversity-in-unity of the Chinese nation assumes that the two levels of identity, national and ethnic, do not replace each other, nor contradict each other, but coexist and co-develop along with linguistic and cultural diversity."[569]

The 1990s saw China putting a high priority on rapid economic development, but concentrating that development predominantly in Han, eastern regions. This left the western, predominately minority regions, underdeveloped, with increased ethnic tension.[570] The Chinese government also sought to curb political power of minority groups by preventing power seizures. In 2001, revisions to the PRC *Law on Autonomy for Minority Regions* and its *Common Language Law* took away some political power and promoted a unitary national language but widened opportunities presented by "positive policies in education, employment, and business opportunities."[571] It is in this period that China set more explicit targets for minority education. In 1993, the government announced three goals for the state education system: compulsory nine-year education for eighty-five percent of the population by 2000, a five to six-year compulsory education for the remaining population living in poverty level areas, and opportunities for a college education for at least eight percent of the population ages eighteen to twenty-one.[572] In 2001, the government added the goal that nine-year education should be implemented in poverty level areas

565 Hill and Zhou, "Introduction," in Hill and Zhou, *Affirmative Action in China and the U.S.*, 8.

566 Sautman, "Affirmative Action, Ethnic Minorities and China's Universities," 77.

567 Hill and Zhou, "Introduction," in Hill and Zhou, *Affirmative Action in China and the U.S.*, 8–9.

568 Ibid.

569 Ibid.

570 Ibid. at 11.

571 Ibid. at 12–13.

572 Ibid. at 15.

as well.[573] The 2001 revision to the PRC Law on Autonomy in Minority Regions, described in greater detail below, also created preferential educational policies for minority students in their current form.

In 2001, the Chinese People's Congress passed the revised PRC Law on Autonomy for Minority Regions.[574] This law created positive policies in education by creating new policies that: "cover[ed] minority school budgets, diversified schooling approaches, lowered admission standards for minority students, increased scholarship awards for them, and created more career opportunities for minority students after graduation."[575]

State-sponsored preferential policies apply to geographic areas with a high concentration of minorities and to individual minority students.[576] Preferential policies in education consist of preferential admissions, lowered school fees, boarding schools, and remedial programs/intervention programs.[577] Many of the preferential admission policies focus on adding points to minority students' entrance exam scores and introducing quotas that reserve a certain percentage of spaces for minority students.[578] Many leading universities hold yearlong preparatory courses for minority students in advance of their entrance exams.[579] Universities located in minority autonomous regions are allowed to teach in minority languages, can administer their own entrance exam, and are not required to use the national level examinations.[580]

There is evidence that preferential policies have meaningfully increased the enrollment of minority students. By 2007, the Yunnan Province had, through preferential policies, increased minority student enrollment to thirty-two percent of all students, a percentage close to their proportion in the province's population.[581] Despite their being admitted with lower scores, on average, minority students reportedly graduate at the same or higher rates as Han

573 Ibid.

574 Ibid. at 13.

575 Ibid.

576 Sautman, "Affirmative Action, Ethnic Minorities and China's Universities," 78.

577 Ibid. at 79.

578 Ibid. at 93–94, 99–101; Wang, "Preferential Policies for Minority College Admission in China: Recent Developments, Necessity, and Impact," in Hill and Zhou, *Affirmative Action in China and the U.S.*, 72–73.

579 Sautman, "Affirmative Action, Ethnic Minorities and China's Universities," 85; Postiglione, "China's National Minorities and Educational Change," 39.

580 Postiglione, "China's National Minorities and Educational Change," 38.

581 Yanchun Dai and Changjiang Xu, "Yunnan's Preferential Policies in Minority Education since the 1980s: Retrospect and Prospects," in *Affirmative Action in China and the U.S.: A Dialogue on Inequality and Minority Education*, ed. Ann Maxwell Hill and Minlang Zhou (New York: Palgrave MacMillan 2009), 108.

students.[582] As a result, many "minorities in China actively seek this benefit and "Han" people seek to be reclassified as minorities."[583]

Preferential policies in education have become controversial in China, with controversy over these programs beginning to mirror arguments made in the United States about the fairness and effectiveness of the policies.[584] Critics report that Han people who live in rural areas and have a similar lack of local educational resources as compared with their minority neighbors see preferential policies as particularly unfair.[585] While they are members of the majority ethnic group, they do not feel they receive the same advantages as Han residents of urban communities and so should not be prevented from receiving preferential treatment.[586] They argue that preferential policies should consider not only ethnic identity, but also regional economic development or individual socioeconomics, believing that minorities living in cities have just as much access to education resources as their Han neighbors.[587] In 2016, in response to the rising pressure, the Ministry of Education required that local education system review and reduce the scope of their affirmative action programs.[588] As of 2017, this has resulted in Beijing limiting bonus points for minority high school students who had emigrated from specifically identified provinces, the Xinjiang Uyghur Autonomous Region no longer receiving 50 bonus points, and Shandong completely eliminating bonus points for minority students.[589]

Students from remote and minority communities remain the most supportive of the current policies. They tend to feel very positively about the program's current structure and cite its usefulness in closing the huge gap in achievement between minorities and the Han.[590]

---

582 Sautman, "Affirmative Action, Ethnic Minorities and China's Universities," 104 (Sautman cites that the preferences, preparatory classes, and tutoring are the main reasons for the government's high retention rates of minority students).

583 Sautman, "Affirmative Action, Ethnic Minorities and China's Universities," 104; Teng and Ma, "Preferential Policies for Ethnic Minorities and Educational Equality in Higher Education in China," in Hill and Zhou, *Affirmative Action in China and the U.S.*, 86.

584 Hill and Zhou, "Introduction," in Hill and Zhou, *Affirmative Action in China and the U.S.*, 2.

585 Ibid. at 1–2.

586 Teng and Ma, "Preferential Policies for Ethnic Minorities and Educational Equality in Higher Education in China," in Hill and Zhou, *Affirmative Action in China and the U.S.*, 88.

587 Ibid.

588 Shan Jie, Several regions to eliminate gaokao points for minorities, Global Times (April 4. 2017), http://www.globaltimes.cn/content/1043439.shtml.

589 Ibid.

590 Teng and Ma, "Preferential Policies for Ethnic Minorities and Educational Equality in Higher Education in China," in Hill and Zhou, *Affirmative Action in China and the U.S.*, 88.

2.7 *Positive Measures in Higher Education – Conclusion*

The preceding discussion of affirmative action in education in Brazil, China, France, India, South Africa and the United States demonstrates the breadth of the movement for positive measures to admit minority students into higher education. In every instance, there is opposition, and the policies are controversial. And in each instance, there are measurable successes, and substantial inequality that justify continuing measures. Some systems use race/ethnicity openly (India, Brazil, South Africa – sometimes the United States and China). Some use region or neighborhood as a substitute (France – sometimes the United States and China). Some include poverty as an added factor, or wealth as a disqualifying one. All but the United States and France use quotas, although the reserved spaces set aside for minority students in India and South Africa are often unfilled. But the differences pale beside the similarities; in these six nations, representing approximately half the world's population, a majority – as identified by race and/or ethnicity – has adopted policies that recognize that a minority population (except in the case of South Africa), again identified by race and/or ethnicity, has been unfairly disadvantaged by their racial/ethnic identity, and is attempting to remedy that disadvantage by taking positive/affirmative/corrective measures/action to provide greater opportunities to members of the minority group for admission into higher education, the principal pathway in our times to wealth and power.

Part 3: Parity Democracy – State Legislative Bodies

In many parts of the world, the national legislature, and in some cases local government, is subject to a system of gender-based (and occasionally race, ethnic, language, and religion-based) proportional representation. Through a variety of different procedures, legislative places are reserved, or systems are created to encourage the election of women or minority group members. Approaches vary from outright quotas to incentives for political parties to nominate more women or minority group members for office. For example, in its weakest form, the United States Democratic Party requires that half of the delegates to its national convention be women.[591]

---

591 Lisa Schnall, "Party Parity: A Defense of the Democratic Party Equal Division Rule," *Journal of Gender, Social Policy & the Law* 13, no. 2 (2005): 381.

Scores of nations around the world provide that half of the seats of the legislature, or a minimum number of seats, are reserved for women. For example, in Africa, there are three main quota systems.[592] The first are constitutional quotas in which constitutional provisions reserve certain national parliament seats for women.[593] The second are systems that require that a certain percentage of the candidates running for Parliament are women, without guaranteeing that that same percentage will win seats.[594] The third are political party quotas in which parties "adopt internal rules to include a certain percentage of women as candidates for office."[595] Countries with political party quotas include South Africa[596] and Mozambique.[597] Fourteen African countries have national legislative seats reserved for women: Algeria, Burundi, Djibouti, Eritrea, Kenya, Morocco, Niger, Somalia, South Sudan, Sudan, Swaziland, Tanzania, Uganda, and Zimbabwe.[598] Another fourteen African countries have legislative candidate quotas: Angola, Burkina Faso, Cape Verde, Democratic Republic of Congo, Egypt, Guinea, Lesotho, Libya, Mauritania, Republic of the Congo, Rwanda, Senegal, Togo, and Tunisia.[599]

In Asia, eight states have national legislative seats reserved for women: Afghanistan, Bangladesh, China, Iraq, Jordan, Pakistan, Saudi Arabia, and Taiwan.[600] Another eight Asian countries have legislative candidate quotas: Armenia, Indonesia, Republic of Korea, Kyrgyzstan, Mongolia, Nepal, Timor-Leste, and Uzbekistan.[601] However, there are also countries in Asia where there are no women in the legislature. Qatar and Yemen have no female representation within their respective legislatures.[602]

---

592 Gumisai Mutume, "Women Break into African Politics: Quota Systems Allow More Women to Gain Elected Office," *African Recovery* 18, no. 1 (2004): 4. http://www.un.org/africarenewal/magazine/april-2004/women-break-african-politics.

593 Ibid.

594 Eilís Ward, "Real or Illusory Progress?: Electoral Quotas and Women's Political Participation in Tanzania, Eritrea, and Uganda," *Trócaire Development Review* (2006): 76. https://www.trocaire.org/sites/default/files/resources/policy/2006-real-illusionary-progress.pdf.

595 Mutume, "Women Break into African Politics: Quota Systems Allow More Women to Gain Elected Office," 4.

596 Ibid.

597 Ibid.

598 "Gender Quotas Database," *International IDEA*. Accessed February 28, 2017. https://www.idea.int/data-tools/data/gender-quotas/database.

599 Ibid.

600 Ibid.

601 Ibid.; In addition, the State of Palestine, whose status as a state remains contested, has candidate quotas for its legislature, the Palestinian Legislative Council.

602 "Proportion of seats held by women in national parliaments (%)," *World Bank Group*. Accessed February 23, 2018. https://data.worldbank.org/indicator/SG.GEN.PARL.ZS.

Argentina adopted the world's first gender quota election law in 1991. Now, all American countries except Canada, the United States, Venezuela, and Guatemala have adopted some form of gender quota laws.[603] Argentina, Bolivia, Brazil, Colombia, Costa Rica, Dominican Republic, Ecuador, El Salvador, Guyana, Honduras, Mexico, Nicaragua, Panama, Paraguay, Peru, and Uruguay have legislated candidate quotas that require parties to run gender-balanced candidate lists.[604] Haiti has reserved seats in the national legislature for women.[605] In 2011, Columbia passed Law 1475 providing for a 30% quota for political parties' election lists, thus building on its prior precedent to establish greater equality in the political sphere as well."[606]

Twenty-two European countries have candidate quotas, which take the form of either legislative quotas wherein each party is required by law to ensure a certain percentage of their candidates are women, or party quotas where the party makes a voluntary commitment to have a certain percentage of their candidates be women.[607] Albania, Belgium, Bosnia, Ireland, Macedonia, Moldova, Montenegro, Poland, and Serbia have only legislative quotas.[608] Austria, Cyprus, Czech Republic, Germany, Hungary, Iceland, Italy, Lithuania, Luxembourg, Malta, The Netherlands, Norway, Romania, Slovakia, Sweden, Switzerland, and The United Kingdom have only party quotas.[609] Croatia, France, Greece, Slovenia, and Spain have both legislative and party quotas.[610] Kosovo has national legislative seats reserved for women.[611]

A few states have adopted parity democracy systems to promote racial, religious, language, or ethnic minorities into legislatures or municipal

603 *See* Jennifer M. Piscopo, "States as Gender Equality Activists: The Evolution of Quota Laws in Latin America," *Latin American Politics and Society* 57, no. 3 (2015): 27–49.

604 Ibid.; "Gender Quotas Database."

605 "Gender Quotas Database."

606 Miguel Camilo Ruiz Blanco, "Deputy Permanent Representative of Colombia to the United Nations Colombia's Statement to the Fifty-Sixth Session of the UN Commission on the Status of Women," (Statement, Fifty-Sixth Session of the UN Commission on the Status of Women, NY, March 15, 2013). http://www.un.org/womenwatch/daw/csw/csw56/general-discussions/member-states/Colombia%20-%20E.PDF.

607 Drude Dahlerup and Lenita Freidenvall, "Electoral Gender Quotas and Their Implementation in Europe," European Parliament, June 2013, accessed February 10, 2019. http://www.europarl.europa.eu/RegData/etudes/note/join/2013/493011/IPOL-FEMM_NT(2013)493011_EN.pdf.

608 "Gender Quotas Database."

609 Ibid.

610 Ibid.

611 Ibid.

councils. In 1993, Colombia adopted Law 70 (the Law of Black Communities).[612] Among the changes introduced were two new, additional, special seats in the House of Representatives for Afro-Colombians and a similar reservation for Amerindians.

India's Constitution specifically reserves seats for Scheduled Castes and Scheduled Tribes in the lower house of Parliament and in the lower houses of state legislatures.[613] (Recall from the discussion of employment that in *Meera Kanwaria v. Sunita and Others* (2006)[614] a woman from the Rajput caste (a higher caste) married a man from a scheduled caste, and thereafter ran for public office (the municipal counsel), seeking a seat reserved for members of the Scheduled Castes. Although by marrying a member of a Scheduled Caste she had taken on his social status, the Indian Supreme Court held that she was ineligible for the reserved seat, because the reservation was intended to compensate for disadvantages she had not suffered, having been born in a "forward caste.")

New Zealand reserves seats for Māori Polynesians, who occupied the country centuries before Europeans.[615] In Slovenia, one seat is reserved for its Italian minority in Istria and another for the Hungarian minority in Prekmurje.[616] Samoa reserves seats for people of foreign or mixed descent without traditional village ties.[617] Lebanon's parliament was evenly divided between Christians and Muslims for many years.[618] In Jordan, nine seats are reserved for Christians and three for Circassions.[619]

In Russia, "some provincial governments have developed ... quotas for candidates from indigenous peoples into parliaments."[620] In Canada, Denmark, Finland, and Spain, "legislation guarantees parliamentary representation (in the chambers) of autonomous formation or territories densely populated by ethnic groups."[621] Denmark "provides space in the national parliament for two

612 Paschel, "The Right to Difference: Explaining Colombia's Shift from Color Blindness to the Law of Black Communities," 730.

613 INDIA CONST. art. 334.

614 *Meera Kanwaria v. Sunita and Others*, AIR 2006 SC 597, 2006 1 SCC 344.

615 Petra Meier, "Defining Groups Entitled to Reserved Seats in National Legislatures: A Comparative Approach," 4 (meeting paper, American Political Science Association 2009 Annual Meeting, Washington D.C., 2009).

616 Ibid. at 6, 13–14.

617 Ibid. at 5, 13–14.

618 Ibid. at 7, 10, 13–14.

619 Ibid. at 13–10.

620 Kathrin Wessendorf, *An Indigenous Parliament?: Realities and Perspectives in Russia and the Circumpolar North* (Copenhagen: IWGIA, 2005), 15.

621 Ibid. at 32.

persons elected by the Greenlandic population and two by the Faroe Island population."[622] In Hungary, legislation provides "that minorities have the right to be represented in the state assembly."[623] In Poland, "electoral committees of the organizations of national minorities have the right to propose a list of parliamentary candidates without any additional conditions imposed upon them, while the parties of national minorities do not need to reach the threshold of 7% of all votes."[624] In Croatia, "persons belonging to ethnic and national associations or minorities that make up more than 8% of the population of the Republic have the right to be represented proportional to their population numbers in the Assembly and government, as well as higher organs of the judiciary; if the minority population makes up less than 8%, they can have five deputies elected to the Chamber of Representatives of the Assembly as representatives of all ethnic and national associations or minorities, and they are obliged to protect their interests."[625]

Should legislative quotas be regarded as a violation of the formal equality principal? The French Constitutional Council (which serves as a Constitutional Court) rejected legislation in 1982 that required at least 20% of the National Assembly seats be reserved for women on the ground that it violated the principal of formal equality, by dividing French citizens into categories of male and female.[626] But when the French Parliament subsequently redrafted the legislation to provide that women constituted half of the whole of France, and political parties should thus be required to reserve half the places on their candidate lists for women, the Council approved the legislation.[627]

Part 4: Positive Measures and Corporate Boards

4.1 *Background*

Although sex discrimination in employment has been illegal in most parts of the world for many years, a "glass ceiling" has kept women noticeably underrepresented in top executive positions and on corporate boards across the

622 Ibid. at 15.
623 Ibid. at 32.
624 Ibid.
625 Ibid.
626 *See* Darren Rosenblum, "Parity/Disparity: Electoral Gender Inequality on the Tightrope of Liberal Constitutional Traditions," *U.C. Davis Law Review* 39, no. 3 (2006): 1119, 1140.
627 Ibid. at 1141–1143.

world.[628] Europe is the leader in implementing positive measures to address the corporate board issue.[629] Among countries that have the highest percentage of women on corporate boards are Norway, France, and Sweden.[630] At the other end of the spectrum, countries with the lowest gender parity on corporate boards include Taiwan and South Korea.[631]

Within Europe, there is nearly a twenty-three-percentage point difference between the average percentage of women on boards in Norway (the highest) and Switzerland (the lowest). These differences are substantially driven by the introduction of quotas and soft regulatory measures at the national level, as well as perhaps differing perceptions on the importance of board gender diversity in individual European states.[632]

There are two common approaches that governments utilize to achieve corporate board gender parity: "hard laws" and "soft laws." Hard quota laws mandate a specific level of representation for corporate boards that must be reached over a specified number of years.[633] These may apply to only state-owned enterprises or public bodies, or to state-owned enterprises, public bodies, and publicly traded limited liability companies.[634] Soft laws include regulations or policies that "may urge or recommend, with varying degree of forcefulness, that companies meet certain predetermined representation levels."[635]

4.2 *Hard Law Positive Measures and Corporate Boards*

Countries that have adopted quotas, but limited them to state or publicly owned bodies, include Colombia, Finland, Greece, Kenya, and Slovenia.[636]

---

628 Aaron A. Dhir, *Challenging Boardroom Homogeneity: Corporate Law, Governance, and Diversity* (New York: Cambridge University Press, June 23, 2016): 3.

629 Ibid.

630 *The CS Gender 3000: The Reward for Change* (Zurich: Credit Suisse AG, September 2016): 8. https://evolveetfs.com/wp-content/uploads/2017/08/Credit-Suisse-Reward-for-Change_1495660293279_2.pdf.

631 Ibid.

632 European Women on Boards, *Gender Diversity on European Boards – Realizing Europe's Potential: Progress and Challenges* (Brussels: European Women on Boards, April 2016): 19. http://www.femmes-experts-comptables.com/wp-content/uploads/2016/07/EWOB-Press-Kit_Final_060716.pdf.

633 Dhir, *Challenging Boardroom Homogeneity*, 74.

634 Ibid.

635 Ibid. at 72.

636 Ibid. at 74; Deloitte Global Center for Corporate Governance, "Women in the Boardroom, A Global Perspective," 17, 39, 51, 55. Accessed November 12, 2018. https://www2.deloitte.com/content/dam/Deloitte/global/Documents/Risk/Women%20in%20the%20boardroom%20a%20global%20perspective%20fifth%20edition.pdf.

The list of countries with hard laws that also apply to private, publicly traded limited liability companies, is longer. It includes Belgium, France, Germany, India, Israel, Italy, Malaysia, the Netherlands, and Norway.[637] Israel was the earliest adopter of a hard quota law, requiring equal representation of both genders on the boards of state-owned companies in 1993.[638] Quotas in Colombia, Greece, and Norway have been in place since before 2005.[639] The remaining hard quota laws have all been passed since 2010, signaling a steady and increasing attention to corporate board representation.[640]

The European Commission proposed a directive in 2012 to increase women's presence on the boards of the major European publicly listed companies to forty percent by 2020. The directive has not yet been adopted, and the target was included in the EU's report on "Strategic Engagement for Gender Equality 2016–2019" as an 'ongoing' priority with no deadline.[641]

Norway was the first country to implement mandatory gender quotas for privately owned, publicly traded companies.[642] It consistently leads the world in the percentage of board seats held by women, at forty-two percent.[643] Its success has garnered considerable praise and scholarly attention, and the conclusion that "Norway's consistently high level of female board membership can be attributed to … Norway's mandatory quota on board gender diversity."[644]

The Norwegian Public Limited Companies Act No. 45 of 1997, as amended in 2003, imposes quota requirements for appointing board members of certain limited liability companies.[645] If a company fails to comply with the quotas, the Register of Business Enterprise provides two warnings. For each warning,

637 Dhir, *Challenging Boardroom Homogeneity*, 74; "Women in the Boardroom, A Global Perspective," 24, 28, 46, 52, 53, 59, 61, 62, 74.

638 "Women in the Boardroom, A Global Perspective," 74.

639 Ibid. at 17, 55, 62 (Norway's law has been in effect since 2005. Statutes in Colombia and Greece were passed in 2000).

640 "Women in the Boardroom, A Global Perspective," 24, 28, 46, 52, 53, 59.

641 *Proposal for a Directive of the European Parliament and of the Council on improving the gender balance among non-executive directors of companies listed on stock exchanges and related measure*, COM (2012) 614 final (Nov. 11, 2012). Accessed November 12, 2018. https://eur-lex.europa.eu/legal-content/EN/TXT/PDF/?uri=CELEX:52012PC0614&from=EN; European Commission, *Strategic Engagement for Gender Equality 2016–2019*, Luxembourg: Publications Office of the European Union, 2015. doi:10.2838/454429.

642 Dhir, *Challenging Boardroom Homogeneity*, 76–77.

643 "Women in the Boardroom, A Global Perspective," 79.

644 European Women on Boards, *Gender Diversity on European Boards*, 19.

645 Anne Kjølseth Ekerholt, Advokatfirmaet Selmer, and Carmen Di Marino, "Norway," in *Paul Hastings, LLP, "Breaking the Glass Ceiling: Women in the Boardroom,"* 3rd ed., eds. Tara Giunta and Lianne Labossiere (Los Angeles: Paul Hastings LLP, 2013), 94–95.

the company has a month to comply with the quota. If the company fails to fulfill the quota requirement, the court will order the dissolution of the company.[646]

In December 2005, the government made the quota rule mandatory for public limited liability companies.[647] Enactment of the regulation commenced on January 1, 2006.[648] Companies registering before the 2006 deadline had two years to comply with the quota rule requirements.[649] Companies seeking registration were required to comply with the quota regulation in order to register.[650] Therefore, for new companies, failure to comply with the quotas could mean a denial of registration.[651]

The Norwegian Gender and Equality Act was another initiative enacted to promote gender parity.[652] The Act includes guidelines for increasing gender representation in public and private sector organizations that are not limited liability companies.[653] The most recent version of the Gender Equality Act includes a call for equal representation for "publicly appointed boards, councils, and committees."[654] The Act provides the following examples: a board comprising of 2–3 members must have at least 1 minimum representation of each gender.[655] A board comprising of 4–5 members requires at least 2 minimum representation of each gender.[656] A board with 6–8 members requires at least 3 minimum representation of each gender.[657] Finally, boards with more than nine members require at least forty percent minimum representation of each gender.[658]

646 Ibid.

647 Ibid. at 96.

648 Ibid.

649 Ibid.

650 Ibid.

651 Ibid.

652 Catherine Seierstad and Morten Huse, "Gender Quotas on Corporate Boards in Norway: Ten Years Later and Lessons Learned," in *Gender Diversity in the Boardroom Vol. 1*, eds. Catherine Seierstad, Patricia Gabaldon, Heike Mensi-Klarbach (Basingstoke: Palgrave Macmillan, 2017), 16.

653 Ibid.

654 Seierstad and Huse, "Gender Quotas," 17; Norway. The Ministry of Children and Equality, *Gender Equality Act*, Oslo: The Ministry of Children and Equality, 2007, Section 13. https://www.regjeringen.no/en/dokumenter/the-act-relating-to-gender-equality-the-/id454568/.

655 Norway. The Ministry of Children and Equality, *Gender Equality Act*, Oslo: The Ministry of Children and Equality, 2007, Section 13. https://www.regjeringen.no/en/dokumenter/the-act-relating-to-gender-equality-the-/id454568/.

656 Ibid.

657 Ibid.

658 Ibid.

Norway's cultural and political commitment to egalitarianism has resulted in increased support of quota laws for gender parity in corporate settings.[659] Though there was considerable debate and controversy over the quota laws when they were first enacted,[660] support among directors has increased as the law has been implemented.[661] In a study surveying Norwegian corporate directors, most responded that "quota-induced gender diversity has positively affected boardroom work and firm governance."[662] They reported that women contribute positively to firms by bringing a range of perspectives and experience, independence, outsider status, and a greater propensity to engage in "rigorous deliberation, risk assessment and monitoring."[663] Furthermore, women did not report feeling stigmatized by quota laws.[664]

Worldwide, there has been a measurable increase in the number of women serving as corporate directors. The Credit Suisse Research Institute, in a study of 27,000 senior managers from 3,000 of the largest global companies, found a fifty-four percent increase in female representation at the Board of Directors level since 2010.[665] In 2015, female board member representation reached 14.7 percent worldwide.[666]

In Europe, the percentage of women on the boards of large European companies went from 13.9 to 25 percent between 2011 and 2015.[667] Five out of the twelve largest European states have mandatory quota requirements for female representation:[668] Belgium, France, Germany, Italy, and Norway.[669] Countries with the highest level of female representation growth between 2011 and 2015 include: Italy (grew by 20.4 percent),[670] Belgium (grew by 16.2 percent),[671] and France (grew by 16.2 percent).[672]

Through SB 826, California became the first state in the United States to require companies based within its borders to put female directors on their

---

659 Dhir, *Challenging Boardroom Homogeneity*, 101.

660 Ibid. at 113.

661 Ibid. at 101.

662 Ibid.

663 Ibid.

664 Ibid. at 102.

665 Credit Suisse, *The CS Gender 3000: The Reward for Change*, 2.

666 Ibid. at 4.

667 European Women on Boards, *Gender Diversity on European Boards – Realizing Europe's Potential*, 10.

668 Ibid. at 10–12.

669 Ibid.

670 Ibid. at 12.

671 Ibid.

672 Ibid.

corporate boards.[673] SB 826 requires that all California Corporations have at least one woman on their board by the end of 2019, and by 2021, companies with at least five directors would need to have two or three female directors, depending on the size of the board, or be fined.[674] However, the bill will likely face constitutional challenges.[675]

At the time of this writing, corporate board hard quota laws exist to promote gender representation only, with no known hard quotas for members of racial or ethnic minority groups.

4.3 *Soft Law Positive Measures and Corporate Boards*

"Soft laws" encompass measures in which governments "may urge or recommend, with varying degree of forcefulness, that companies meet certain predetermined representation levels."[676] These laws most commonly come in the form of disclosure requirements, in which companies are required to report their efforts to increase diversity on their boards or in management. Diversity under these disclosure laws is often not limited to gender, but encompasses broader diversity efforts, including race, ethnicity, LGBT status, and religion.[677]

The United States is among countries that use disclosure as an incentive for companies to increase diversity. In 2009, the Securities and Exchange Commission, the key regulating entity of the public trading of stock shares of United States corporations, issued a rule requiring companies to disclose whether and how diversity is considered in determining corporate board membership.[678] Former SEC Chairwoman Mary Jo White has criticized companies' compliance with this requirement as largely "vague" and ineffective at increasing corporate board diversity.[679] Nonetheless, she has noted that

673 *Vanessa Fuhrmans*, "California Becomes First State to Mandate Female Board Directors," *The Wall Street Journal.* Accessed November 12, 2018. https://www.wsj.com/articles/california-becomes-first-state-to-mandate-female-board-directors-1538341932.

674 Ibid.

675 Joseph A. Grundfest, "Mandating Gender Diversity in the Corporate Boardroom: The Inevitable Failure of California's SB 826," *Rock Center for Corporate Governance at Stanford University Working Paper No. 232* (2018): 2–4. Accessed November 12, 2018. https://ssrn.com/abstract=3248791.

676 Dhir, *Challenging Boardroom Homogeneity*, 72.

677 *See generally*, "Women in the Boardroom, A Global Perspective."

678 17 C.F.R. §§ 229, 239, 240, 249, 274 (2009); Mary Jo White, "Keynote Address, International Corporate Governance Network Annual Conference: Focusing the Lens of Disclosure to Set the Path Forward on Board Diversity, Non-GAAP, and Sustainability," (International Corporate Governance Network Annual Conference San Francisco, California, June 27, 2016). https://www.sec.gov/news/speech/chair-white-icgn-speech.html.

679 White, "Keynote Address."

"a growing number of company proxy statements have recently begun to voluntarily provide an analysis of data, accompanied by pie charts and bar graphs, to describe the state of the board's gender, race and ethnic diversity composition, sometimes in addition to other categories – that is one of the positive results of private ordering."[680] Near the end of her tenure, Ms. White advocated for more stringent SEC disclosure requirements that would model these data-driven voluntary statements as best practices.[681]

Canada has a transparency initiative somewhat similar to that in the United States. Securities regulatory authorities in each Canadian province have, since October 2014, required the corporate entities they regulate to include within their Disclosure of Corporate Governance Practices the following on an annual basis:

- director term limits and other mechanisms of renewal of the board of directors,
- policies regarding the representation of women on the board,
- the board's or nominating committee's consideration of the representation of women in the director identification and selection process,
- the issuer's consideration of the representation of women in executive officer positions when making executive officer appointments,
- targets regarding the representation of women on the board and in executive officer positions, and
- the number of women on the board and in executive officer positions.[682]

In December 2016, the Canadian Government released proposed regulations that would require similar disclosures for entities regulated by the Canada Business Corporations Act.[683] In addition, entities would be required to disclose diversity efforts regarding diversity other than gender.[684]

680 Ibid.

681 Ibid.

682 Canada. Canadian Securities Administrators. *Multilateral CSA Notice of Amendments to National Instrument 58-101*, Montreal: Canadian Securities Administrators, 2014. http://www.osc.gov.on.ca/documents/en/Securities-Category5/csa_20141014_58-101_noa-national-instrument.pdf.

683 "Women in the Boardroom, A Global Perspective," 10.

684 David E. Woollcombe, et al., "Canadian Securities Regulatory Monitor, Proposed Regulations to Bill C-25 Have Now Been Released, and They Add Clarity to Contemplated Changes to Majority Voting, Notice-and-Access Procedures and Diversity Disclosure for Public Corporations Governed by the Canada Business Corporations Act," *Mccarthy Tétrault LLP*, December 19, 2016, accessed April 11, 2018. https://www.securitiesregulationcanada.com/2016/12/proposed-regulations-to-bill-c-25-have-now-been-released-and

Chile, Spain, India, Hong Kong, and Kenya are among additional countries utilizing this disclosure approach.[685] There is some evidence that soft laws have a positive effect on the number of women represented. In the United States, the ratio of women on the boards of companies listed in the Russell 3000 Index has risen from 13.6 percent in 2014 to 15.2 percent in 2016.[686]

The European Union Council adopted a transparency initiative in 2014. Under Directive 2014/95/EU, large companies must publish reports on the policies they implement in relation to ... diversity on company boards (in terms of age, gender, educational and professional background).[687] The requirements are as follows:

> Article 20 – Corporate Governance Statement:
>
> 1. Undertakings referred to in point (1)(a) of Article 2 shall include a corporate governance statement in their management report. That statement shall be included as a specific section of the management report and shall contain at least the following information: "... (g) a description of the diversity policy applied in relation to the undertaking's administrative management and supervisory bodies with regard to aspects such as, for instance, age, gender, or educational and professional backgrounds, the objectives of that diversity policy, how it has been implemented and the results in the reporting period. If no such policy is applied, the statement shall contain an explanation as to why this is the case."[688]

In Denmark, organizations and companies must set specific targets to improve gender representation on boards.[689] The government recommends that

-they-add-clarity-to-contemplated-changes-to-majority-voting-notice-and-access -proceduresand-diversity-disclosure-for-public-corporations/.

685 *See* "Women in the Boardroom, A Global Perspective," 16, 23, 24, 39, 68.

686 "Gender Parity on Boards Around the World," *Harvard Law School Forum on Corporate Governance and Financial Regulation*, accessed November 12, 2018, https://corpgov.law.harvard.edu/2017/01/05/gender-parity-on-boards-around-the-world/.

687 "Non-financial reporting: EU rules require large companies to publish regular reports on the social and environmental impacts of their activities." *European Commission*. Accessed April 11, 2018. https://ec.europa.eu/info/business-economy-euro/company-reporting-and-auditing/company-reporting/non-financial-reporting_en.

688 DIRECTIVE 2014/95/EU OF THE EUROPEAN PARLIAMENT AND OF THE COUNCIL of 22 October 2014 amending Directive 2013/34/EU as regards disclosure of non-financial and diversity information by certain large undertakings and groups, 2014 O.J. (L330) 1.

689 Dhir, *Challenging Boardroom Homogeneity*, 73.

boards consider gender diversity as a factor when vetting potential candidates. However, the government does not impose any set quotas or sanctions for failing to meet targets.[690]

Other forms of incentivizing diversity in corporate board composition include offering recognition to those companies who reach a certain percentage of minority or female representation. Colombia, though it uses hard quotas to promote the representation of women, considered using such recognition incentives to increase racial diversity. "In 2012, the ministry of the Interior proposed a law that would improve the participation and representation of Afro-Colombians in Colombian society ... The legislation would have created ['among other things'] a "Certificate of Ethnic Responsibility" which would be awarded to all private and public companies who employed at least 10% minorities. The proposal was not enacted."[691] In Spain, companies were required beginning in 2007 to present financial statements showing that they "endeavored" to reach an equal representation of men and women (at least 40 percent and no more than 60 percent of one gender).[692] The law did not offer any sanctions for failure to comply. Rather, the law provided awards for companies that comply with the recommendation.[693] But, as of 2014, companies must now set minimum targets on their boards for women on their boards.[694]

Advocacy campaigns on the part of coalitions of corporations, governments, NGOs, and non-profits, have been influential as well in areas that do not use hard laws. In the United States, national campaigns, like 2020 Women on Boards and the Thirty Percent Coalition, may have contributed to the increase in the representation of women on corporate boards without the implementation of mandatory affirmative action policies.[695] And in Brazil, where the government is still discussing whether to implement a quota law, NGOs "are working on projects to improve diversity in Brazil."[696]

---

690 Ibid. at 74.

691 Colombian Ministry of the Interior, *PROYECTO DE LEY ESTATUTARIA No ___ de 2012*. Bogota: Ministry of the Interior, 2012. Accessed November 12, 2018. "Negras, Afrocolombianas, Raizales y Palenqueras," http://www.mininterior.gov.co/sites/default/files/noticias/por_el_cual_se_establece_la_ley_de_participacion_y_representacion_para_las_comunidades_negras_afrocolombianas_raizales_y_palenqueras.pdf.

692 Constitutional Act 3/2007 of 22 March for Effective Equality Between Women and Men, arts. 75, 78 (Spain); Dhir, *Challenging Boardroom Homogeneity*, 73.

693 Constitutional Act 3/2007 of 22 March for Effective Equality Between Women and Men, art. 50 (Spain); Dhir, *Challenging Boardroom Homogeneity*, 73.

694 "Women in the Boardroom, A Global Perspective," 68.

695 "Gender Parity on Boards Around the World."

696 "Women in the Boardroom, A Global Perspective," 15.

In sum, "[i]t is apparent that having a law requiring some mandatory minimum level of female board representation is effective in causing companies to bring female directors on at a rate that satisfies those legal requirements. It is also clear that countries without regulation tend to lag behind those with both hard and soft laws."[697] However, success for such policies is also related to the business culture.[698] For example, Sweden has not enacted a quota law but has higher success rates for gender parity on boards when compared to other nations.[699]

Part 5: Conclusion – The Global Ubiquity of Positive Measures

As noted in the introduction, a full discussion of comparative positive measures must begin, if only briefly, with the world-wide revolution of the late eighteenth through mid-nineteenth centuries, which brought us movements to end slavery, grant universal suffrage, end colonialism, grant equal rights to women and men regardless of social status or property, eliminate the caste system, adopt measures of proportional representation, embrace the benefits of diversity, and endorse universal equality. What a time!

In the years that followed we saw many efforts to remedy the inequalities of the past through proportional representation, quotas, and other special measures. These accelerated after the Second World War and the horror of the Holocaust, as international conventions embraced special measures and substantive equality as an alternative to formal equality.

By the twenty-first century, around the globe we see special measures used to remedy inequality in employment, access to higher education, political participation, and representation in corporate decision-making. Nearly every large nation in the world has adopted at least some special measure plans, with continuing experiments using quotas, reservations, set-asides, reparations, preferences, tie-breakers, targeted recruiting efforts, diversity measures, equity and inclusion policies, anti or unconscious bias training, and public disclosure requirements.

But all the progress of the post-War period is in peril. Around the globe, right-wing politicians have used positive measures as a wedge issue to turn their supporters against equality rights for minority racial, ethnic and religious

697 "Gender Parity on Boards Around the World."

698 Ibid.

699 Ibid.

groups, minority sexual identity groups, women, migrants, and people with disabilities. There is no guarantee of progress.

It is thus critical that we extend our vision and compare our own national approaches to remedying inequality to those of our neighbors, and beyond. In my experience, when we examine our own national policies in isolation, the argument that they offend principals of formal equality seem to have greater force. When we recognize how broadly substantive equality policies are embraced – how ubiquitous positive measures policies are globally – our perspective shifts. I hope that reading this work has helped my readers shift their perspective, as writing it has for me.

Acknowledgements

I am very grateful to Professor Laura Carlson, the general editor of this series, for bringing together such a remarkable group of authors, and for including me among them. I am also very grateful to my Berkeley Law research assistants, Chelsea Breana Davis, Class of 2019, Daniella V. Hernandez, Class of 2018, Katie Lee, Class of 2019, Nicole Mauri, Class of 2019, Alexis Payne, Class of 2019, Anu Ramdin, class of 2021 and Edward Richter, Class of 2020, and to Julia Herrmann. For a better understanding of affirmative action and the Roma, I am grateful to Dr. Jozefien Caeneghem. For a better understanding of reservations in India, I am grateful to Shivangi Misra, Legal Officer with the Lawyers Collective, Delhi, India. I've consulted with many members of the Berkeley Comparative Equality and Anti-Discrimination Law Study Group, a very supportive community of scholars and legal activists. Finally, I am beyond grateful to my wife Marcy, whose love sustains me.

Bibliography

17 C.F.R. §§ 229, 239, 240, 249, 274 (2009).

37th U.S. Congress. *Statutes at Large of the United States (1863–1865)*. Washington: Library of Congress, 1864.

84/635/EEC: Council recommendation of 13 December 1984 on the promotion of positive action for women, 1984 OJ (L 331).

"A Brief History of Employment Equity in Canada," *Public Service Alliance of Canada.com*. February 2, 2017. Accessed October 29, 2017. http://psacunion.ca/brief-history-employment-equity-canada.

Abrams, Morris B. "Affirmative Action: Fair Shakers and Social Engineers," *Harvard Law Review* 99, no. 6 (1986): 1312–1346.

Adarand Constructors, Inc. v. Pena, 115 S. Ct. 2097 (1995).

"Affirmative Action in Colombia: Debating Quotas," *The Economist*. July 30, 2009. Accessed October 29, 2017. http://www.economist.com/node/14140625.

AIR 1995 SC 1648: (1995) 4 SCC 520.

"Alphabetical List of ILO Member Countries," *ILO.Org*. October 22, 2018. Accessed November 11, 2018, https://www.ilo.org/public/english/standards/relm/country.htm.

Andrews, George Reid. "Brazilian Racial Democracy, 1900–90: An American Counterpoint," *Journal of Contemporary History* 31, no. 3 (1996): 483–507.

Archibong, Uduak and Oluyinka Adejumo. "Affirmative Action in South Africa: Are we Creating New Casualties?" *Journal of Psychological Issues in Organizational Culture* 3, no. S1 (2013): 14–27.

Badat, Saleem and YuSuf Sayed. "Post-1994 South African Education: The Challenge of Social Justice," *The Annals of the American Academy* 652 (March 2014): 127–148.

Badek, CJEU Case C-158/97.

Bailey, Stanley R. *Legacies of Race Identities, Attitudes, and Policies in Brazil*. Stanford: Stanford University Press, 2009.

Banton, Michael. "National Integration in France and Britain," *Journal of Ethnic and Migration Studies* 27, no. 1 (2001): 152–166. doi:10.1080/13691830124752.

Barnay, Thomas, Emmanuel Duguet, Christine Le Clainche, and Yann Videau. "An evaluation of the 1987 French Disabled Workers Act: Better paying than hiring," *hal-01260162* (2016). https://hal.archives-ouvertes.fr/hal-01260162/document.

Bell, Mark. *Racism and Equality in the European Union*. (Oxford: Oxford University Press, 2009). Oxford Scholarship Online, 2009. doi:10.1093/acprof:oso/9780199297849.001.0001.

Bentley, George R. *A History of the Freedmen's Bureau*. Philadelphia: University of Pennsylvania Press, 1955.

"Berea College Early History," *Berea College*. Accessed January 12, 2018. https://www.berea.edu/about/history/.

Bernardino-Costa, Joaze and Ana E. Blackman. "Affirmative Action in Brazil and Building an Anti-racist University," *Race Ethnicity and Education* 20, no. 3 (2017): 372–384. http://dx.doi.org/10.1080/13613324.2016.1260228.

Bhatia, Gautam. "Caste and the Law," *India Law ejournal* 15, no. 12 (2019): 1–10. Accessed February 22, 2019. https://papers.ssrn.com/sol3/papers.cfm?abstract_id=3325812.

Biller, David. "Bolsonaro Says Black Brazilians Aren't Owed Anything Over Slavery," *Bloomberg.com*. July 31, 2018, https://www.bloomberg.com/news/articles/2018-07-31/brazil-candidate-bolsonaro-minimizes-slavery-praises-trump.

"Black History Month: A Medical Perspective: Education," *LibGuides*. Accessed December 21, 2017. http://guides.mclibrary.duke.edu/blackhistorymonth/education.

Blanco, Miguel Camilo Ruiz. "Deputy Permanent Representative of Colombia to the United Nations Colombia's Statement to the Fifty-Seventh Session of the UN Commission on the Status of Women," Statement, Fifty-Seventh Session of the UN Commission on the Status of Women, NY, March 15, 2013.

Blanco, Miguel Camilo Ruiz. "Deputy Permanent Representative of Colombia to the United Nations Colombia's Statement to the Fifty-Sixth Session of the UN Commission on the Status of Women," Statement, Fifty-Sixth Session of the UN Commission on the Status of Women, NY, March 9, 2012.

Bostdorff, Denise M. and Steven R. Goldzwig, "History, Collective Memory, and the Appropriation of Martin Luther King, Jr.: Reagan's Rhetorical Legacy," *Presidential Studies Quarterly* 35, no. 4 (2005): 661–690.

Branch, Taylor. *Parting the Waters: America in the King of Years 1954–63*. New York: Touchstone, 1989.

Bridges, Khiara M. "The Deserving Poor, the Undeserving Poor, and Class-Based Affirmative Action," *Emory Law Journal* 66 (2017): 1049–1114.

Brief of Harvard University, Brown University, The University of Chicago, Dartmouth College, Duke University, The University of Pennsylvania, Princeton University, and Yale University as Amici Curiae Supporting Respondents, *Grutter v. Bollinger*, 2003 WL 399220 (U.S. Feb. 8, 2003).

Brink v. Kitshoff (1996) 4 SALJ 197 (CC).

Brown, Kevin D. and Sitapati, Vinay, "Lessons Learned from Comparing the Application of Constitutional Law and Federal Anti-Discrimination Law to African-Americans in the U.S. and Dalits in India in the Context of Higher Education," *Harvard Blackletter Law Journal* 24 (2008): 3–59.

Brown, Michael K., Martin Carnoy, Elliott Currie, Troy Duster, David B. Oppenheimer, Marjorie M. Shultz, and David Wellman, *Whitewashing Race: The Myth of a Color-Blind Society*. Berkeley: University of California Press, 2003.

Brown-Nagin, Tomiko. "Rethinking Proxies for Disadvantage in Higher Education: A First Generation Students' Project," *University of Chicago Legal Forum* 1 (2014): 433–500.

Bryant, Lisa. "Survey: Blacks in France Say They Face Racial Discrimination," *Voice of America News*, February 2, 2007.

C-158/97, Georg Badeck and others, 2000 ECR I-1875 (2000).

C-409/95, *Marschall v. Land Nordrhein-Westfalen*, 1997 ECR I-6363 (1997).

C-450/93, *Kalanke v. Freie Hansestadt*, 1995 ECR I-3051 (1995).

CAL. CONST., art. I, § 31.

Canada. Canadian Securities Administrators. *Multilateral CSA Notice of Amendments to National Instrument 58-101*, Montreal: Canadian Securities Administrators, 2014. http://www.osc.gov.on.ca/documents/en/Securities-Category5/csa_20141014_58-101_noa-national-instrument.pdf.

Canadian Charter of Rights and Freedoms, Part I of the *Constitution Act, 1982*, being Schedule B to the *Canada Act 1982* (UK), 1982, c 11. Accessed October 29, 2017. http://laws-lois.justice.gc.ca/eng/Const/page-15.html.

Carlson, Laura. *Comparative Discrimination Law: Historical and Theoretical Frameworks*. Leiden: Brill, 2017. doi:10.1163/9789004345454.

CESCR, General Comment No. 5: Persons with Disabilities, E/1995/22 (December 9, 1994).

CESCR, General Comment No. 16: The Equal Right of Men and Women to the Enjoyment of All Economic, Social and Cultural Rights (Art. 3 of the Covenant), E/C.12/2005/4, (August 11, 2005).

CESCR Committee, CESCR, General Comment No. 20 (Non-Discrimination in Economic, Social and Cultural Rights (Art. 2, para. 2 of the ICESCR), UN Doc. E/C.12/GC/20 (July 2, 2009).

Chambers, Frederick. "Histories of Black Colleges and Universities," *Journal of Negro History* 57, no. 3 (July 1972): 270–275.

City of Richmond v. J.A. Croson Co., 488 U.S. 469 (1989).

Clancy, Patrick and Gaële Goastellec. "Exploring Access and Equity in Higher Education: Policy and Performance in a Comparative Perspective," *Higher Education Quarterly* 61, no. 2 (2007):136–154.

CN v. Canada (Canadian Human Rights Commission), [1987] 1 S.C.R. 1114 (Can.).

Cole, Alistair, Patrik Le Galès, and Jonah D. Levy, eds. *Developments in French Politics 4*. Houndsmills, Basingstoke, Hampshire and New York: Palgrave Macmillan, 2008.

Collins, Sharon M. "The Making of the Black Middle Class," *Social Problems* 30, no. 4 (1983). https://doi.org/10.2307/800108.

Commission on Equality in Employment, *Equality in Employment: A Royal Commission*, Ottawa: Minister of Supply and Services Canada, 1984. Accessed October 29, 2017. http://crrf-fcrr.com/images/stories/Equality_in_Employment.pdf.

Conseil Constitutionnel [CC] [Constitutional Court] Decision No. 2001-450 cd.-July 11, 2001, J.O. 11506. https://www.conseil-constitutionnel.fr/decision/2001/2001450DC.htm.

Constitutional Act 3/2007 of 22 March for Effective Equality Between Women and Men (Spain).

The Constitutional Council. *Decision No. 2007-557 DC November 15th 2007*. Paris: The Constitutional Council, 2017. https://law.yale.edu/system/files/documents/pdf/Intellectual_Life/Decision_No.2007–557_DC_November_15th_2007.pdf.

Constitucion Politica De Colombia [C.P.], art. 1.

"The Constitution: The Certification Process," *Constitutional Court of South Africa*. Accessed February 23, 2018. http://www.constitutionalcourt.org.za/site/the constitution/thecertificationprocess.htm.

Constituicao Federal [C.F.] [Constitution] art. 113, § 1 (Braz.).

Constituicao Federal [C.F.] [Constitution] art. 122, § 1 (Braz.).

Constituicao Federal [C.F.] [Constitution] art. 141, § 1 (Braz.).

Constituicao Federal [C.F.] [Constitution] art. 3 (Braz.).

Constituicao Federal [C.F.] [Constitution] art. 5 (Braz.).

Colombian Ministry of the Interior, PROYECTO DE LEY ESTATUTARIA No ___ de 2012. Bogota: Ministry of the Interior, 2012. Accessed November 12, 2018. "Negras, Afrocolombianas, Raizales y Palenqueras," http://www.mininterior.gov.co/sites/default/files/noticias/por_el_cual_se_establece_la_ley_de_participacion_y_representacion_para_las_comunidades_negras_afrocolombianas_raizales_y_palenqueras.pdf.

Convention on the Elimination of All Forms of Discrimination Against Women (CEDAW), 18 December 1979, 1249 U.N.T.S. 13.

Convention on the Rights of Persons with Disabilities: resolution / adopted by the General Assembly, 24 January 2007, 2515 U.N.T.S. 3, A/RES/61/106.

The CS Gender 3000: The Reward for Change. Zurich: Credit Suisse AG, September 2016. https://evolveetfs.com/wp-content/uploads/2017/08/Credit-Suisse-Reward-for-Change_1495660293279_2.pdf.

Council Directive 2000/43/EC of 29 June 2000 implementing the principle of equal treatment between persons irrespective of racial or ethnic origin, 2000 OJ (L 180).

Council Directive 2000/78/EC of 27 November 2000 establishing a general framework for equal treatment in employment and occupation, 2000 OJ (L 303).

Council Directive 2014/95/EU (EC).

Council Directive 76/207/EEC of 9 February 1976 on the implementation of the principle of equal treatment for men and women as regards access to employment, vocational training and promotion, and working conditions, Feb. 9, 1976, 1976 O.J. (L 39).

Council of Europe, *Advisory Committee on the Framework Convention for the Protection of National Minorities, First Opinion on Serbia and Montenegro*, Strasbourg: Council of Europe, 2003, ACFC/INF/OP/I (2004)002.

Council of Europe, *The Situation of Roma in Europe and Relevant Activities of the Council of Europe*, Parliamentary Assembly, June 22, 2010, accessed February 15, 2019. http://assembly.coe.int/nw/xml/XRef/Xref-XML2HTML-en.asp?fileid=17875&lang=en.

The Council on Higher Education. "Postgraduate Studies in South Africa: A Statistical Profile," *Higher Education Monitor*, no. 7 (March 2009). http://www.che.ac.za/sites/default/files/publications/CHE_MonitorProjectV7.pdf.

Cultural India. "Life History of Shahu Chhatrapati," *Biography – Life History, Facts, Achievements & Death*. May 15, 2016, accessed January 18, 2019. https://www.culturalindia.net/reformers/shahu-chhatrapati.html.

Cunningham, Clark D. "Affirmative Action: India's Example," *Civil Rights Journal*. (1999): 22–27.

Dahlerup, Drude, and Lenita Freidenvall, "Electoral Gender Quotas and Their Implementation in Europe," *European Parliament*, June 2013, accessed February 10, 2019. http://www.europarl.europa.eu/RegData/etudes/note/join/2013/493011/IPOL-FEMM_NT(2013)493011_EN.pdf.

Dai, Yanchun and Changjiang Xu. "Yunnan's Preferential Policies in Minority Education since the 1980s: Retrospect and Prospects," in *Affirmative Action in China and the U.S.: A Dialogue on Inequality and Minority Education*, edited by Ann Maxwell Hill and Minlang Zhou, 99–118. New York: Palgrave MacMillan, 2009.

Déclaration du 26 août 1789 des droits de l'homme et du citoyen. [French Declaration of Human and Civic Rights]. CONSEIL CONSTITUTIONNEL [CONSTITUTIONAL COUNCIL], Aug. 26, 1789; CONST (Fr.).

DeFunis v. Odegaard, 82 Wash. 2d 11 (1973).

Deloitte Global Center for Corporate Governance, "Women in the Boardroom, A Global Perspective," accessed November 12, 2018. https://www2.deloitte.com/content/dam/Deloitte/global/Documents/Risk/Women%20in%20the%20boardroom%20a%20global%20perspective%20fifth%20edition.pdf.

Department of Education. *White Paper on Education & Training*, Cape Town: Department of Education, 1995, accessed February 14, 2018. https://www.education.gov.za/Portals/0/Documents/Legislation/White%20paper/White%20paper%20on%20Education%20and%20Training%201995.pdf?ver=2008-03-05-111656-000.

Deshpande, Ashwini. *Affirmative Action in India*. Oxford: Oxford University Press, 2013.

Deslippe, Dennis. *Protesting Affirmative Action: The Struggle over Equality after the Civil Rights Revolution*. Baltimore: Johns Hopkins University Press, 2012.

Dewitt, Larry. "The Decision to Exclude Agricultural and Domestic Workers from the 1935 Social Security Act," *Social Security Bulletin* 70, no. 4 (2010).

Dhir, Aaron A. *Challenging Boardroom Homogeneity: Corporate Law, Governance, and Diversity*. New York: Cambridge University Press, 2016.

Directive 2000/43/EC of 29 June 2000.

Directive 2000/78/EC of 27 November 2000.

DIRECTIVE 2014/95/EU OF THE EUROPEAN PARLIAMENT AND OF THE COUNCIL of 22 October 2014 amending Directive 2013/34/EU as regards disclosure of non-financial and diversity information by certain large undertakings and groups, 2014 O.J. (L330).

Dischino, Christopher. "Affirmative Action in Brazil: Reverse Discrimination and the Creation of a Constitutionally Protected Color-Line," *University of Miami International and Comparative Law Review* 155 (2014): 155–190.

"Diversity Charters in Europe," Diversity Journal, August 28, 2012, accessed February 10, 2019. http://www.diversityjournal.com/9762-diversity-charters-in-europe/.

Domingo, Pilar, Alina Rocha Menocal, Verónica Hinestroza, "PROGRESS DESPITE ADVERSITY: Women's empowerment and conflict in Colombia," (London: developmentprogress.org, 2015). https://www.odi.org/sites/odi.org.uk/files/odi-assets/publications-opinion-files/9743.pdf.

Donahoo, Saran. "Reflections on Race: Affirmative Action Policies Influencing Higher Education in France and the United States," *Teachers College Record* 110, no. 2 (February 2008): 251–277.

Ekerholt, Anne Kjølseth, Advokatfirmaet Selmer, and Carmen Di Marino. "Norway," in *Paul Hastings, LLP, "Breaking the Glass Ceiling: Women in the Boardroom,"* 3rd ed., eds. Tara Giunta and Lianne Labossiere, 94–97. Los Angeles: Paul Hastings LLP, 2013.

Espinosa, Manuel José Cepeda and David Lanau. *Colombian Constitutional Law: Leading Cases*. Oxford: Oxford University Press, 2017.

"EU Platform of Diversity Charters," *The European Commission*, August 1, 2018, accessed February 10, 2019. https://ec.europa.eu/info/policies/justice-and-fundamental-rights/combatting-discrimination/tackling-discrimination/diversity-management/eu-platform-diversity-charters_en.

European Agency for Fundamental Rights, "Roma Internship," *European Agency for Fundamental Rights*, accessed November 11, 2018. http://fra.europa.eu/en/vacancy/2017/roma-internship-programme-2017-2018.

European Commission against Racism and Intolerance (ECRI), *General Policy Recommendation No. 7: National Legislation to Combat Racism and Racial Discrimination*. Strasbourg: ECRI, 2017.

European Commission Communication The interpretation of the judgment of the Court of Justice on 17 October 1995 in Case C-450/93, *Kalanke v. Freie Hansestadt Bremen*, COM (96) 88 final.

European Commission. *Strategic Engagement for Gender Equality 2016–2019*. Luxembourg: Publications Office of the European Union, 2015. doi:10.2838/454429.

Exec. Order No. 9980, 3 C.F.R. (1948).

Exec. Order. No. 10925, 26 FR 1977 (1961).

Exec. Order. No. 11246, 30 FR 12319 (1965).

February, Judith. "From Redress to Empowerment: The New South African Constitution and Its Implementation," In *The Next Twenty-Five Years: Affirmative Action in Higher Education in the United States and South Africa*, edited by David L. Featherman, Marvin Krislov, and Martin Hall, 77–81. Ann Arbor: University of Michigan Press, 2010.

Fisher v. University of Texas at Austin, 133 S. Ct. 2411 (2013).

Fisher v. University of Texas at Austin, 136 S. Ct. 2198 (2016).

Fletcher, Robert Samuel. *A History of Oberlin College from its Foundation Through the Civil War*. Oberlin: Oberlin University Press, 1943.

Foner, Eric. *Reconstruction: America's unfinished revolution, 1863–1877*. New York: Harper Collins, 2011.

Fredman, Sandra. "Emerging from the Shadows: Substantive Equality and Article 14 of the European Convention on Human Rights," *Human Rights Law Review* 16, no. 2 (2016): 273–301. doi:10.1093/hrlr/ngw001.

Fuhrmans, Vanessa. "California Becomes First State to Mandate Female Board Directors," *The Wall Street Journal*. Accessed November 12, 2018. https://www.wsj.com/articles/california-becomes-first-state-to-mandate-female-board-directors-1538341932.

Garrison, William A., and Andre Modigliani. "The changing culture of affirmative action," In *Equal employment opportunity: labor market discrimination and public policy*, edited by Paul Burstein, 373–393. New York: Aldine Transaction, 1994.

Galanter, Marc. *Competing Equalities: Law and the Backward Classes in India*. Berkeley: University of California Press, 1984.

Gender Diversity on European Boards – Realizing Europe's Potential: Progress and Challenges. Brussels: European Women on Boards, April 2016. http://european.ewob-network.eu/wp-content/uploads/2016/04/EWoB-quant-report-WEB-spreads.pdf.

"Gender Parity on Boards Around the World," *Harvard Law School Forum on Corporate Governance and Financial Regulation*. January 5, 2017, accessed November 12, 2018. https://corpgov.law.harvard.edu/2017/01/05/gender-parity-on-boards-around-the-world/.

"Gender Quotas Database," *International IDEA*. Accessed February 28, 2017. https://www.idea.int/data-tools/data/gender-quotas/database.

Ghadyalpatil, Abhiram. "Rajarshi Shahu Chhatrapati of Kolhapur, a Reformer Ahead of His Time," *Livement.com*. August 10, 2018, accessed January 18, 2019. https://www.livemint.com/Leisure/PLkr7jdpCeZepho8RMVJbN/Rajarshi-Shahu-Chhatrapati-of-Kolhapur-a-reformer-ahead-of.html.

Govt. of A.P v. P.B Vijayakumar 1995 4 SCC 520.

Gratz v. Bollinger, 539 U.S. 244 (2003).

Gregory, James N. *The Southern Diaspora: How the Great Migrations of Black and White Southerners Transformed America*. Chapel Hill: University of North Carolina Press, 2006.

Grundfest, Joseph A. "Mandating Gender Diversity in the Corporate Boardroom: The Inevitable Failure of California's SB 826," *Rock Center for Corporate Governance at Stanford University Working Paper No. 232* (2018). Accessed November 12, 2018. https://ssrn.com/abstract=3248791.

Grutter v. Bollinger, 539 U.S. 306 (2003).

Hand, James, Bernard Davis, and Pat Feast. "Unification, simplification, amplification? An analysis of aspects of the British Equality Act 2010," *Commonwealth Law Bulletin* 38, no. 3 (2012): 509–528.

Haney López, Ian. *Dog Whistle Politics: How Coded Racial Appeals Have Reinvented Racism and Wrecked the Middle Class*. New York: Oxford University Press, 2014.

Hansen-Bundy, Benjy. "Afro-Colombians battle racism and socio-economic exclusion," *Colombia Reports*. March 22, 2013, accessed October 29, 2017. https://colombiareports.com/afro-colombians-battle-racism-and-socio-economic-exclusion/.

Hare, Thomas. *Election of Representatives, Parliamentary and Municipal*. 4th ed. London: Longmans, Green, Reader, & Dyer, 1873.

Hernández, Tanya K. "Affirmative Action in the Americas," *Americas Quarterly*. 7, no. 3 (2013): 26–32. Accessed Nov. 11, 2018. https://www.americasquarterly.org/affirmative-action-in-the-americas.

High Court of South Africa. *In the High Court of South Africa (Cape of Good Hope Provincial Division), Cape Town: Tuesday 1 March 2005, Third Division: Court No. 16*. Cape Town: High Court of South Africa, 2005, accessed February 10, 2018. https://www.westerncape.gov.za/other/2005/3/high_court_roll_1-4march05.pdf.

Hill, Ann Maxwell and Minglang Zhou, eds. *Affirmative Action in China and the U.S.: A Dialogue on Inequality and Minority Education*. New York: Palgrave Macmillan, 2009.

"The Honourable Rosalie Silberman Abella," *Supreme Court of Canada*. October 2, 2017, accessed October 29, 2017. http://www.scc-csc.ca/judges-juges/bio-eng.aspx?id=rosalie-silberman-abella.

Htun, Mala. "From 'Racial Democracy' to Affirmative Action: Changing State Policy on Race in Brazil," *Latin American Research Review* 60, no. 1 (2004): 60–89. https://doi.org/10.1353/lar.2004.0010.

Hughes v. Superior Court, 339 U.S. 460 (1950).

INDIA CONST. amend. XCIII.

INDIA CONST. art. 15, § 4.

INDIA CONST. art. 16.

International Convention on the Elimination of All Forms of Racial Discrimination, 21 December 1965, 94 U.T.S. 1120, 660 U.N.T.S. 195.

International Covenant on Economic, Social and Cultural Rights, 16 December 1966, 993 U.N.T.S. 3.

International Labour Office, *ABC of Women Workers' Rights and Gender Equality*. Geneva: International Labour Organisation, 2000.

International Labour Organization (ILO), Constitution of the International Labour Organisation (ILO). April 1, 1919.

International Labour Organization (ILO), ILO Declaration on Fundamental Principles and Rights at Work, June 1988.

Johnson, Lyndon B. "To Fulfill These Rights," Speech, Howard University Commencement Address, Howard University, Washington D.C., June 4, 1965.

Johnson v. Transportation Agency, 480 U.S. 616 (1987).

Johnson III, Ollie A., and Rosana Heringer, eds. *Race, Politics, and Education in Brazil.* New York: Palgrave Macmillan, 2015. doi:10.1057/9781137485151.

Jones, Faustine C. "Black Americans and the City: A Historical Survey," *Journal of Negro Education* 42, no. 3 (1973): 261–282.

Kalev, Alexandra, Erin Kelly, and Frank Dobbin, "Best Practices or Best Guesses? Assessing the Efficacy of Corporate Affirmative Action and Diversity Policies," *American Sociological Review* 71, (2006): 589–617.

Kelly, Erin, and Frank Dobbin. "How affirmative action became diversity management: Employer response to antidiscrimination law, 1961 to 1996," *American Behavioral Scientist* 41, no. 7 (1998): 960–984.

Kennedy, Randall. *For Discrimination: Race, Affirmative Action, and the Law.* New York: Penguin Random House, 2013.

Kersch, Ken I. *Constructing civil liberties: Discontinuities in the development of American constitutional law*. Cambridge: Cambridge University Press, 2004.

"Key Events in Black Higher Education: JBHE Chronology of Major Landmarks in the Progress of African Americans in Higher Education," *Journal of Blacks in Higher Education*. Accessed January 12, 2018. https://www.jbhe.com/chronology/.

Kotlowski, Dean J. *Nixon's Civil Rights: Politics, Principle, & Policy*. Cambridge: Harvard University Press, 2009.

Kotlowski, Dean J. "Richard Nixon and the Origins of Affirmative Action," *The Historian* 60, no. 3 (1998): 523–541.

Krishnan, P.S. and Vasanti Devi. *A Crusade for Social Justice; Bending Governance towards the Deprived.* Chennai: South Vision Books, 2017.

"La Charte De La Diversité," Charte De La Diversité | Charte De La Diversité. 2018. Accessed February 10, 2019. https://www.charte-diversite.com/charte-de-la-diversite/.

Langan, Elise S. "Assimilation and Affirmative Action in French Education Systems," *European Education* 40, no. 3 (2008): 49–64.

Lee, Christopher J. "Mourning Mandela," *Transition*, no. 116 (2014): 167–171.

Lempp, Sarah. "Jair Bolsonaro and Affirmative Action: Political Rupture or Escalation?" Allegra. April 2, 2019, accessed May 15, 2019. http://allegralaboratory.net/jair-bolsonaro-and-affirmative-action-political-rupture-or-escalation/.

Levine, Robert S. *Martin R. Delany: A Documentary Reader*. Chapel Hill: University of North Carolina Press, 2003.

Lindsay, Beverly. "Toward Conceptual, Policy, and Programmatic Frameworks of Affirmative Action in South African Universities," *The Journal of Negro Education* 66, no. 4 (1997): 522–538.

Loi n° 87-517 du 10 juillet 1987 en faveur de l'emploi des travailleurs handicapés [Law No. 87-517 of 10 July 1987 on the employment of disabled workers] Journal Officiel De La Republique Francaise [J.O.] [Official Gazette of France], July 12, 1987.

Londoño, Ernesto, and Shasta Darlington. "Jair Bolsonaro Wins Brazil's Presidency, in a Shift to the Far Right," *The New York Times*. October 28, 2018, accessed February 3, 2019. https://www.nytimes.com/2018/10/28/world/americas/jair-bolsonaro-brazil-election.html.

Lozes, Patrick. Interview with David B. Oppenheimer, Personal Interview, Paris: France, March 28, 2014.

Martins, Sérgio Da Silva, Carlos Alberto Medeiros and Elisa Larkin Nascimento. "Paving Paradise: the Road from 'Racial Democracy' to Affirmative Action in Brazil." *Journal of Black Studies* 34, no. 6 (2004): 787–816.

Martin, Waldo E. and Patricia Sullivan, "'Don't Buy Where You Can't Work' Campaigns," *U.S. History in Context*. Accessed 29 Oct. 2017. link.galegroup.com/apps/doc/BT2338230739/UHIC?u=k12_histrc&xid=8c8bd1b6.

McCrudden, Christopher. "A Comparative Taxonomy of 'Positive Action' and 'Affirmative Action' Policies," *Queen's University Belfast Law Research Paper* 12, no. 4 (2012): 157–180.

McCrudden, Christopher, Raya Muttarak, Heather Hamill, and Anthony Heath. "Affirmative action without quotas in Northern Ireland," *The Equal Rights Review* 4, (2009): 7–14. http://www.equalrightstrust.org/ertdocumentbank/err_issue04%20christopher.pdf.

McDonald v. Santa Fe Trail Transp., 427 U.S. 273 (1976).

Meera Kanwaria v. Sunita and Others, AIR 2006 SC 597.

Meier, August, and Elliott Rudwick. "The Origins of Nonviolent Direct Action in Afro-American Protest: A Note on Historical Discontinuities," in *Along the Color Line: Explorations in the Black Experience*, edited by David Levering Lewis, 307–405. Champaign: University of Illinois Press, 1976.

Meier, Petra. "Defining Groups Entitled to Reserved Seats in National Legislatures: A Comparative Approach," Meeting paper, American Political Science Association 2009 Annual Meeting, Washington D.C., 2009.

MICH. CONST., art. I, § 26.

Mill, John S. *Considerations on Representative Government*. London: Parker, Son, & Bourn, 1861.

Minister of Finance and another v. Van Heerden 2004 (6) SA 123 (CC).

Ministry of Law and Justice. *The Rights of Persons with Disabilities Act, 2016*. New Delhi: Gazette of India (Extra-Ordinary). Accessed Feb. 24, 2018. http://www.upfcindia.com/documents/rpwd_101017.pdf.

Ministry of Social Justice and Empowerment, *The Constitution (One Hundred and Twenty Fourth Amendment) Bill, 2019*. New Delhi: PRS Legislative Research, 2019. Accessed February 22, 2019. https://www.prsindia.org/billtrack/constitution-one-hundred-and-twenty-fourth-amendment-bill-2019.

Mitra, Amrita. "Affirmative Action for Women in Indian Constitution," August 15,2012, accessed November 11, 2018. http://dx.doi.org/10.2139/ssrn.2129663.

Moreno, Paul. "An Ambivalent Legacy: Black Americans and the Political Economy of the New Deal," *The Independent Review* 6, no. 4 (2002): 513–539.

Motala and Another v. University of Natal 1995 (3) BCLR 374 (D).

M.R. Balaji v. State of Mysore, AIR 1963 SC 649.

Mutume, Gumisai. "Women Break into African Politics: Quota Systems Allow More Women to Gain Elected Office," *African Recovery* 18, no. 1 (2004). http://www.un.org/africarenewal/magazine/april-2004/women-break-african-politics.

NAACP v. Claiborne Hardware Co., 458 U.S. 886 (1982).

Naff, Katherine C. and Frederik Uys. "Representative Bureaucracy in South Africa: Success or Failure," Paper presented to the annual meeting of the Midwest Political Science Association, April 7–10, 2005, Chicago.

Nagpur Today. "Meritorious X, XII Students Honoured by BSP," Nagpur Today Nagpur News RSS. July 27, 2015, accessed January 18, 2019. https://www.nagpurtoday.in/meritorious-x-xii-students-honoured-by-bsp/07271411.

National Assembly. *Act Respecting Equal Access to Employment in Public Bodies*, A-2.01. Quebec: Legis Quebec, 2001. Accessed October 29, 2017. http://legisquebec.gouv.qc.ca/en/ShowDoc/cs/A-2.01.

National Education Policy Act 27 of 1996 (S. Afr.). http://www.puk.ac.za/opencms/export/PUK/html/fakulteite/opvoed/mediasentrum/Dokumente/godsdiensonderwysbeleid.pdf.

New Negro Alliance v. Sanitary Grocery Co., 303 U.S. 552 (1938).

"Non-financial reporting: EU rules require large companies to publish regular reports on the social and environmental impacts of their activities." *European Commission*. Accessed April 11, 2018. https://ec.europa.eu/info/business-economy-euro/company-reporting-and-auditing/company-reporting/non-financial-reporting_en.

Norway. The Ministry of Children and Equality, *Gender Equality Act*, Oslo: The Ministry of Children and Equality, 2007. https://www.regjeringen.no/en/dokumenter/the-act-relating-to-gender-equality-the-/id454568/.

Nugent, Ciara. "How Far-Right Populist Jair Bolsonaro Could Transform Brazil," *Time*. October 25, 2018, accessed February 3, 2019. http://time.com/5433379/brazil-bolsonaro-policies/.

O'Cinneide, Colm. "The European Social Charter and the UK: Why it Matters," *King's Law Journal* 29, no. 2, (2018): 275–296. https://doi.org/10.1080/09615768.2018.1502064.

Olsen, Jesse E. and Luis L. Martins, "Understanding organizational diversity management programs: A theoretical framework and directions for future research," *Journal of Organizational Behavior* 33, no. 8 (2012): 1168–1187.

Oppenheimer, David B. "Distinguishing Five Models of Affirmative Action," *Berkeley Women's Law Journal* 4, no. 1 (1988): 42–61.

Oppenheimer, David B. "Archibald Cox and the Diversity Justification for Affirmative Action," *Virginia Journal of Social Policy and the Law* 25, no. 2, (2018): 157–203.

Oppenheimer, David B. "Color-Blindness, Racism-Blindness, and Racism-Awareness: Revisiting Judge Henderson's Proposition 209 Decision," *Berkeley Journal of African American Law & Policy* 12 (2011): 229–256.

Oppenheimer, David Benjamin. "Understanding Affirmative Action," *Hastings Const. LQ* 23 (1995): 921–997.

Oppenheimer, David B. "The Disappearance of Voluntary Affirmative Action from the U.S. Workplace," *Journal of Poverty and Social Justice* 24, no. 1 (2016): 37–50.

Oppenheimer, David B. et al. *Comparative Equality & Anti-Discrimination Law*, 2nd ed. Berkeley: Comparative Equality Press, 2017.

Oppenheimer, David B. "Dr. King's Dream of Affirmative Action," *Harvard Latinx Law Review* 21 (2018): 55–86.

Osborn, Marilyn, Patricia Broadfoot, Claire Planel, and Andrew Pollard. "Social Class, Educational Opportunity and Equal Entitlement: Dilemmas of Schooling in England and France," *Comparative Education* 33, no. 3 (1997): 375–393.

Osorio, Rafael Guerreiro. "The Persistence of Black-White Income Differentials in Brazil," In *Affirmative Action in Plural Societies: International Experiences*, edited by Graham K. Brown, Arnim Langer, and Frances Stewart, 119 New York: Palgrave Macmillan, 2012.

Pandey, Balaji. "Educational Development among Scheduled Castes," *Social Scientist* 14, no. 2/3 (1986): 59–68.

Parents Involved in Community Schools v. Seattle School District No. 1, 551 U.S. 701 (2007).

Parikh, Sunita. *The Politics of Preference: Democratic Institutions and Affirmative Action in the United States and India.* Ann Arbor: University of Michigan Press, 1997.

Parker, Stephen, Kalervo N. Gulson, and Trevor Gale, eds. *Policy and Inequality in Education.* Glasgow and Sydney: Springer, 2017.

Paschel, Tianna S. "The Right to Difference: Explaining Colombia's Shift from Color Blindness to the Law of Black Communities," *American Journal of Sociology* 116, no. 3 (2010): 729–769.

Pauley, Garth E. "Harry Truman and the NAACP: A Case Study in Presidential Persuasion on Civil Rights," *Rhetoric and Public Affairs* 2, no. 2, Special Issue on Civil Rights in the Postmodern Era (1999): 211–241.

Piscopo, Jennifer M. "States as Gender Equality Activists: The Evolution of Quota Laws in Latin America," *Latin American Politics and Society* 57, no. 3 (2015): 27–49.

Polakow-Suransky, Sasha. "CRÈME DE LA CRÈME," *Legal Affairs*. July/August 2004, accessed February 3, 2019. http://www.legalaffairs.org/issues/July-August-2004/story_suransky_julaug04.msp.

Pons-Vignong, Nicolas and Ward Anseeuw. "Great Expectations: Working Conditions in South Africa since the End of Apartheid," *Journal of Southern African Studies* 35, no. 4 (2009): 883–899.

Postiglione, Gerard A. "China's National Minorities and Educational Change," *Journal of Contemporary Asia* 22, no. 1 (1992): 20–44.

"Proportion of seats held by women in national parliaments (%)," *World Bank Group*. Accessed February 23, 2018. https://data.worldbank.org/indicator/SG.GEN.PARL.ZS.

Proposal for a Directive of the European Parliament and of the Council on improving the gender balance among non-executive directors of companies listed on stock exchanges and related measure, COM (2012) 614 final (Nov. 11, 2012). Accessed November 12, 2018. https://eur-lex.europa.eu/legal-content/EN/TXT/PDF/?uri=CELEX:52012PC0614&from=EN.

"Race and ethnicity in South Africa," *South African History*. Accessed March 21, 2018. http://www.sahistory.org.za/article/race-and-ethnicity-south-africa.

Raman, Sujit M. "Caste in Stone: Consequences of India's Affirmative Action Policies," *Harvard International Review* 21, no. 4 (1999): 30–34.

"The Rights of Persons with Disabilities Act, 2016, Gazette of India (Extra-Ordinary)," accessed December 28, 2016. http://www.disabilityaffairs.gov.in/uploaad/uploadfiles/files/RPWD/ACT/2016.pdf.

Rosenblum, Darren. "Parity/Disparity: Electoral Gender Inequality on the Tightrope of Liberal Constitutional Traditions," *U.C. Davis Law Review* 39, no. 3 (2006): 1119–1189.

Rothstein, Richard. *The Color of Law: A Forgotten History of How Our Government Segregated America*. New York: Liveright, 2017.

Rubio, Philip. *History of Affirmative Action, 1619–2000*. Jackson: University Press of Mississippi, 2001.

Sabbagh, Daniel. "Affirmative Action at Sciences Po," *French Politics, Culture & Society* 20, no. 3 (2002): 52–64. http://www.jstor.org.libproxy.berkeley.edu/stable/42843247.

S. Afr. Const., 1996. section 9.

Sautman, Barry. "Affirmative Action, Ethnic Minorities and China's Universities," *Pacific Rim Law & Policy Journal* 7, no. 1 (January 1998): 77–116.

Savage, Charlie. "Justice Dept. to Take on Affirmative Action in College Admissions," *The New York Times*. August 1, 2017, accessed February 24, 2018. https://www.nytimes.com/2017/08/01/us/politics/trump-affirmative-action-universities.html.

Sawhney v. Union of India, AIR 1993 SC 477.

Sayed, YuSuf, Anil Kanjee, and Mokubung Nkomo. *The Search for Education Quality in Post-Apartheid South Africa: Interventions to Improve Learning and Teaching*. Cape Town: HSRC Press, May 2013.

Schnall, Lisa. "Party Parity: A Defense of the Democratic Party Equal Division Rule," *Journal of Gender, Social Policy & the Law* 13, no. 2 (2005): 381–414.

Senate and House of Commons of Canada. *Employment Equity Act S.C., 1995, c. 44*. Ottowa: Justice Laws Website, 2012. Accessed October 29, 2017. http://laws-lois.justice.gc.ca/eng/acts/e-5.401/page-1.html.

Seierstad, Catherine and Morten Huse. "Gender Quotas on Corporate Boards in Norway: Ten Years Later and Lessons Learned," in *Gender Diversity in the Boardroom Vol. 1*, eds. Catherine Seierstad, Patricia Gabaldon, and Heike Mensi-Klarbach, 11–45. Basingstoke: Palgrave Macmillan, 2017.

Singh v. State of Bihar, 1994 SCC (4) 401.

Skrentny, John D., ed. *Color Lines: Affirmative Action, Immigration, and Civil Rights Options for America*. Chicago and London: The University of Chicago Press, 2001.

South African Parliament, *Employment Equity Act 1998*, Cape Town: Government Gazette, 1998. Accessed November 17, 2017. http://www.labour.gov.za/DOL/downloads/legislation/acts/employment-equity/eegazette2015.pdf.

Srivastava, D. K. "Progress of sexual harassment law in India, China and Hong Kong: prognosis for further reform," *Harvard International Law Journal Online* 51 (2010). http://www.harvardilj.org/2010/08/online_51_srivastava/.

State of Madras v. Dorairajan, AIR 1951 SC 226.

S.T.F., RMS 26.071-1/DF, Relator: Min. Carlos Britto, 13.11.2007, R.S.T.F., 314 (Brazil).

S.T.J., RMS 26.089 PR 2008/0003014-1, Relator: Min. Felix Fischer, 12.05.2008 (Brazil).

S.T.J., RMS 26.089 – PR 2008/0003014-1 (Brazil) (translation by author).

Students for Fair Admissions, Inc. v. President and Fellows of Harvard College, No. 14-cv-14176-ADB (D. Mass. filed Nov. 17, 2014).

Students for Fair Admissions, Inc. v. University of North Carolina, No. 1:14-cv-00954 (D.M.D.N.C. filed Nov. 17, 2014).

Sullivan, Zoe. "'We're Afraid': Advocates Say Brazil's Presidential Frontrunner a Threat to Gay Rights," *NBCNews.com*. October 6, 2018, accessed February 3, 2019. https://www.nbcnews.com/feature/nbc-out/we-re-afraid-advocates-say-brazil-s-presidential-frontrunner-threat-n917111.

Supreme Court, Durban and Coast Local Division 1995 (3) BCLR 374 (D); 1995 SACLR LEXIS 256 JUDGMENT DATE: 24/02/1995.

Supremo Tribunal Federal (Federal Supreme Court of Brazil). *Press Release University of Brasilia Affirmative Action Case, Docket No. ADPF 186*. April 26, 2012.

Sweatt v. Painter, 339 U.S. 629 (1950).

"Table 306.20. Total fall enrollment in degree-granting postsecondary institutions, by level and control of institution and race/ethnicity of student: Selected years, 1976 through 2015," *Digest of Education Statistics, National Center for Education Statistics*. Accessed February 13, 2018. https://nces.ed.gov/programs/digest/d16/tables/dt16_306.20.asp?current=yes.

"Table 313.10. Fall enrollment, degrees conferred, and expenditures in degree-granting historically Black colleges and universities, by institution: 2014, 2015, and 2014–15," *Digest of Education Statistics, National Center for Education Statistics*. Accessed February 13, 2018. https://nces.ed.gov/programs/digest/d16/tables/dt16_313.10.asp?current=yes.

Thakur v. Union of India, (2008) 6 SCC 1.

Thakur v. Union of India, (2007) 4 SCC 361.

Timpson, Anna M. *Driven Apart: Women's Employment Equality and Child Care in Canadian Public Policy*. Vancouver: UBC Press, 2002.

Truman, Harry S. "Special Message to the Congress on Civil Rights," Speech, Washington D.C., February 2, 1948. Accessed February 15, 2018. https://www.trumanlibrary.org/publicpapers/index.php?pid=1380&st=&st1=.

UK Parliament, *Equality Act of 2010*, London: Legislation.gov.uk. Accessed February 21, 2019. https://www.legislation.gov.uk/ukpga/2010/15.

United Steelworkers v. Weber, 443 U.S. 193, 241 (1979).

UN Committee on the Elimination of Racial Discrimination (CERD), General Recommendation no. 32, The meaning and scope of special measures in the International Convention on the Elimination of All Forms [of] Racial Discrimination, 24 September 2009, CERD/C/GC/32.

UN Committee on the Elimination of Racial Discrimination (CERD), Report of the Committee on the Elimination of Racial Discrimination: Seventy-fifth session (3–28 August 2009), 21 December 2011, A/64/18.

UN Committee on the Rights of Persons with Disabilities (CRPD), Concluding observations on the initial report of China, adopted by the Committee at its 8th session, 17–28 September 2012: Committee on the Rights of Persons with Disabilities, 15 October 2012, CRPD/C/CHN/CO/1.

U.S. Const. amend. XIII.

U.S. Const. amend. XIV.

U.S. Department of Education. *Historically Black Colleges and Universities and Higher Education Desegregation*. Washington D.C.: U.S. Dep't of Education Office for Civil Rights, 1991. Accessed February 23, 2019. https://www2.ed.gov/about/offices/list/ocr/docs/hq9511.html.

Valente, Rubia R., and Brian J. Berry. "Performance of Students Admitted through Affirmative Action in Brazil," *Latin American Research Review* 52, no. 1 (2017): 18–34.

Van Caeneghem, Jozefien. *The Use of Ethnic Data Collection and Positive Action to Combat Discrimination and Promote Equality and Social Inclusion of the Roma Minority in Europe*. (PhD diss., Vrije Universiteit Brussel, 2017).

Verwey, Cornel, and Michael Quayle. "Whiteness, Racism, and Afrikaner Identity in Post-Apartheid South Africa," *African Affairs* 111, no. 445 (2012): 551–575.

"Visible Minority and Population Group Reference Guide, National Household Survey, 2011," *Statistics Canada*. December 31, 2015. Accessed October 29, 2017, http://www12.statcan.gc.ca/nhs-enm/2011/ref/guides/99-010-x/99-010-x2011009-eng.cfm.

Voice Of America, "Survey: Blacks in France Say They Face Racial Discrimination," *VOA*. November 1, 2009, accessed February 16, 2019. https://www.voanews.com/a/a-13-2007-02-05-voa27/404117.html.

Waddington, Lisa. "Disability: A Human Rights Issue," *Maastricht Journal of European and Comparative Law* 1, no. 4 (December 1994): 334–336. doi:10.1177/1023263X9400100401.

Waddington, Lisa. "The relationship between Disability Non-Discrimination Law and Quota Schemes: A comparison between Common Law and Civil Law Jurisdictions in Europe," in *Anti-Discrimination Law in Civil Law Jurisdictions*, edited by Barbara Havelkova and Mathias Moschel (Oxford: Oxford University Press, (forthcoming in 2019)).

Wade, Peter. "Defining Blackness in Colombia," *Journal de la Société des Américanistes* 95, no. 1 (2009): 165–184.

Walby, Sylvia. "The European Union and gender equality: Emergent varieties of gender regime," *Social Politics: International Studies in Gender, State & Society* 11, no. 1 (2004): 4–29.

Wang, Tiezhi. "Preferential Policies for Minority College Admission in China: Recent Developments, Necessity, and Impact," in *Affirmative Action in China and the U.S.: A Dialogue on Inequality and Minority Education*, edited by Ann Maxwell Hill and Minlang Zhou, 71–82. New York: Palgrave MacMillan, 2009.

Ward, Eilís. "Real or Illusory Progress?: Electoral Quotas and Women's Political Participation in Tanzania, Eritrea, and Uganda," *Trócaire Development Review* (2006): 73–95. https://www.trocaire.org/sites/default/files/resources/policy/2006-real-illusionary-progress.pdf.

Washington, Tanya Monique. "All Things Being Equal: The Promise of Affirmative Efforts to Eradicate Color-Coded Inequality in the United States and Brazil," *National Black Law Journal* 21, no. 1 (2009): 1–42.

WASH. REV. CODE § 49.60.400 (1998).

"Welcome to the official Truth and Reconciliation Commission Website," *Truth and Reconciliation Commission*. Accessed February 23, 2018. http://www.justice.gov.za/trc/index.html.

Wessendorf, Kathrin. *An Indigenous Parliament?: Realities and Perspectives in Russia and the Circumpolar North*. Copenhagen: IWGIA, 2005.

Wilkerson, Isabel. *The warmth of other suns: The epic story of America's great migration*. New York: Vintage, 2011.

"Whitelash – Neologisms," *The Rice University Neologisms Database*. December 3, 2016, accessed February 24, 2018. http://neologisms.rice.edu/index.php?a=term&d=1&t=20709.

White, Mary Jo. "Keynote Address, International Corporate Governance Network Annual Conference: Focusing the Lens of Disclosure to Set the Path Forward on Board Diversity, Non-GAAP, and Sustainability," International Corporate Governance Network Annual Conference, San Francisco, California, June 27, 2016. https://www.sec.gov/news/speech/chair-white-icgn-speech.html.

"Why India needs a new debate on caste quota," *BBC News*. August 29, 2015, accessed February 2019. http://www.bbc.com/news/world-asia-india-34082770.

World Bank. 2010. *Roma inclusion: An economic opportunity for Bulgaria, Czech Republic, Romania and Serbia (English)*. Washington D.C.: World Bank. http://documents.worldbank.org/curated/en/196921468261335364/Roma-inclusion-An-economic-opportunity-for-Bulgaria-Czech-Republic-Romania-and-Serbia.

Woollcombe, David E. et al. "Canadian Securities Regulatory Monitor, Proposed Regulations to Bill C-25 Have Now Been Released, and They Add Clarity to Contemplated Changes to Majority Voting, Notice-and-Access Procedures and Diversity Disclosure for Public Corporations Governed by the Canada Business Corporations Act," *Mccarthy Tétrault LLP*. December 19, 2016, accessed April 11, 2018. https://www.securitiesregulationcanada.com/2016/12/proposed-regulations-to-bill-c-25-have-now-been-released-and-they-add-clarity-to-contemplated-changes-to-majority-voting-notice-and-access-procedures-and-diversity-disclosure-for-public-corporations/.

Zante, Agnes. "Widening Participation in France and Its Effects on the Field of Elite Higher Education and on Educational Policy," in *Policy and Inequality in Education*, edited by Stephen Parker, Kalervo N. Gulson, and Trevor Gale, 73–89. Glasgow and Sydney: Springer, 2017.

Zhou, Minglang. "Tracking the Historical Development of China's Positive and Preferential Policies for Minority Education: Continuities and Discontinuities," in *Affirmative Action in China and the U.S.: A Dialogue on Inequality and Minority Education*, edited by Ann Maxwell Hill and Minlang Zhou, 47–70. New York: Palgrave Macmillan, 2009.

www.ingramcontent.com/pod-product-compliance
Lightning Source LLC
Chambersburg PA
CBHW022105240926
51848CB00008B/148
9789004345980